3/08

A CONCISE GUIDE TO
Macroeconomics

A CONCISE GUIDE TO
Macroeconomics

What Managers, Executives, and Students Need to Know

David A. Moss

Harvard Business School Press
Boston, Massachusetts

Copyright 2007 David A. Moss
All rights reserved
Printed in the United States of America
11 10 09 08   5 4 3 2

ISBN 13: 978-1-4221-0179-7

Library of Congress cataloging information forthcoming

The paper used in this publication meets the minimum requirements of the American National Standard for Information Sciences—Permanence of Paper for Printed Library Materials, ANSI Z39.48-1992.

For my students

CONTENTS

Contents

ACKNOWLEDGMENTS

This volume began as a note on macroeconomics for my students, and I am deeply indebted to them and to my colleagues in the BGIE unit at Harvard Business School for encouraging me to turn the note into a book. I am particularly grateful to Julio Rotemberg, Dick Vietor, and Lou Wells for reading and commenting on the entire manuscript, and to Alex Dyck, Walter Friedman, Lakshmi Iyer, Andrew Novo, Huw Pill, Mitch Weiss, and Jim Wooten for providing vital feedback along the way, and to all my BGIE colleagues over the years, from whom I have learned so much about macroeconomics and how to teach it.

Jeff Kehoe, my editor at Harvard Business School Press, was extraordinarily supportive at every stage, and offered superb advice on how to recast the original note for a broader audience.

Chapter 5, on GDP accounting, draws heavily on a Harvard Business School case entitled "National Economic Accounting: Past, Present, and Future," which I coauthored with Sarah Brennan. Most of what I know about the intricacies of GDP accounting I learned working with Sarah, and I remain exceedingly grateful to her for her commitment to that project and for being such a terrific researcher, coauthor, and friend.

Finally, I wish to thank my parents, who, in so many ways, inspired this book by teaching me not to lose sight of the big picture; and my wife and daughters—Abby, Julia, and Emily—for their unending support and patience and for making every day so much fun.

Introduction

Macroeconomic forces affect all of us in our daily lives. Inflation rates influence the prices we pay for goods and services and, in turn, the value of our incomes and our savings. Interest rates determine the cost of borrowing and the yield on bank accounts and bonds, while exchange rates affect our command over foreign products as well as the value of our foreign assets. And all of this represents just the tip of the iceberg. Numerous macro variables—ranging from unemployment to productivity—are equally important in shaping the economic environment in which we live.

For most business managers, a basic understanding of macroeconomics allows a more complete—as well as a more nuanced—conception of market conditions, on both the demand side and the supply side. It also ensures that they are better equipped to anticipate and to respond to major macroeconomic events, such as a sudden depreciation of the real exchange rate or steep hike in the federal funds rate.

Although managers can enjoy success even if they don't truly understand these sorts of macro variables, they have the potential to outperform their competitors—to see hidden opportunities and to avoid unnecessary (and sometimes very costly) mistakes—after incorporating basic macro concepts and relationships into their management toolbox. In the 1990s, for example, managers who knew how to read and interpret a balance of payments statement had a definite leg up in dealing with the Mexican and Asian currency crises.

And the practical value of macroeconomics extends beyond the confines of business. A basic understanding of the subject is important to us as consumers, as workers, as investors, and even as voters. Whether our elected officials (and the individuals they appoint to lead crucial agencies, such as the Federal Reserve and the Treasury Department) manage the macro economy well or poorly obviously has great significance for our quality of life, both now and in the future. Whether a large budget deficit is advantageous or disadvantageous at a particular moment in time is something that voters should be able to evaluate for themselves.

Unfortunately, even many well-educated citizens have never studied macroeconomics. And those who have studied the subject too often learned more about how to solve artificial problem sets than about the true fundamentals of the macro economy. Macroeconomics is frequently taught with a heavy focus on equations and graphs, which, for many students, obscure the essential ideas and intuition that make the subject meaningful. This book attempts to provide a conceptual overview of macroeconomics, emphasizing essential principles and relationships, rather than mathematical models and formulas. The purpose is to convey the fundamentals—the building blocks—and to do so in a way that is both accessible and relevant.

The approach employed here is one I have helped to develop over the past decade at Harvard Business School. In fact, I drafted the first version of this book as a primer for my students, and it has since been adopted as required reading in many programs at HBS. Although the approach is quite different from what one would find in a standard macro textbook (graduate or undergraduate), it is an approach that we have found to be very effective and that has also been well received by students and executives alike.

As the remainder of this volume makes clear, macroeconomics may be thought of as resting on three basic pillars: output, money, and expectations. Because output is the central pillar, we begin with that topic in chapter 1 and follow with money and expectations in chapters 2 and 3, respectively. Together, chapters 1 through 3 comprise part I of the book, which covers the fundamentals of macroeconomics in as compact a form as possible.

For readers interested in digging a bit deeper, chapters 4 through 7 (part II) provide more detailed coverage in several key areas. These chapters are not meant to be comprehensive, but rather to address a handful of macro topics that typically provoke the most questions in the classroom. Chapter 4 provides a brief historical survey of U.S. monetary policy, tracing management of the nation's money supply from the dawn of the republic down to the present. Experience suggests that a historical approach proves particularly effective in conveying both the logic and limits of monetary policy and central banking. Chapters 5 and 6 cover the basics of macroeconomic accounting. Just as knowledge of how to read an income statement and a balance sheet is essential for assessing a company, knowledge of how to read a GDP account (chapter 5) and a balance of payments statement (chapter 6) is essential for assessing a country and the performance of its economy. Finally, chapter 7 surveys the topic of exchange rates, focusing on factors that are thought to drive currencies to appreciate or depreciate. Although the path of an exchange rate, like the trajectory of a stock, is notoriously difficult to predict, there are certainly a number of important economic relationships one should take into account when—for either personal or business reasons—a prediction is required.

Unlike a standard textbook, this volume is designed to be read in just a few sittings. Although readers may wish to return to particular sections from time to time (to brush up on exchange rates or fiscal policy, for example), they are likely to get the most out of the book if they first read it (or at least read part I) in its entirety—the goal being to develop a broad understanding of the subject, its key pieces, and how they fit together.

With that in mind, we begin at the conceptual heart of macroeconomics, with an exploration of national output in chapter 1.

I

Understanding the Macro Economy

CHAPTER ONE

Output

The notion of *national output* lies at the heart of macroeconomics. The total amount of output (goods and services) that a country produces constitutes its ultimate budget constraint. A country can use more output than it produces only if it borrows the difference from foreigners. Large volumes of output—not large quantities of money—are what make nations prosperous. A national government could print and distribute all the money it wanted, turning all of its residents into millionaires. But collectively they would be no better off than before unless national output increased as well. And even with all that money, they would find themselves worse off if national output declined.

Measuring National Output

The most widely accepted measure of national output is gross domestic product (GDP). In order to understand what GDP is, it is first necessary to figure out how it is measured.

The central challenge in measuring national output (GDP) is to avoid counting the same output more than once. It might seem obvious that total output should simply equal the value of *all* the goods and services produced in an economy—every pound of steel, every tractor, every bushel of grain, every loaf of bread, every meal sold at a restaurant, every piece of paper, every architectural blueprint, every building constructed, and so forth. But this isn't quite right, because counting *every* good and service actually ends up counting the same output again and again, at multiple stages of production.

A simple example illustrates this problem. Imagine that Company A, a forestry company, cuts trees in a forest it owns and sells the wood to Company B for $1,000. Company B, a furniture company, cuts and sands the wood and fashions it into tables and chairs, which it then sells to a retailer, Company C, for $2,500. Company C ultimately sells the tables and chairs to consumers for $3,000. If, in calculating total output, one added up the sales price of every transaction ($1,000 + $2,500 + $3,000), the result ($6,500) would overstate the amount of output because it would count the value of the lumber three times (in all three transactions) and the value of the carpentry twice (in the final two).

A good way to avoid the over-counting problem is to focus on the value added—that is, the new output created—at each stage of production. If a tailor bought an unfinished shirt for $50, sewed on buttons costing $1, and then sold the finished shirt for $60, we would not say that he *created* $60 worth of output.

Rather, he added $9 of value to the unfinished shirt and buttons, and thus created $9 worth of output. More precisely, value added (or output created) equals the sales price of a good or service minus the cost of all nonlabor inputs used to produce it.

We can easily apply this method to the A-B-C example just given. Because Company A sold the raw wood it had cut for $1,000, and had purchased no material inputs, it added $1,000 of value (output) to the economy. Company B added another $1,500 in value, since it paid $1,000 for inputs (from Company A) and sold its output (to Company C) for $2,500. Finally, Company C added another $500 in value, having purchased $2,500 in inputs (from Company B) and sold $3,000 worth of final output to consumers. If one sums the value added at each stage ($1,000 + $1,500 + $500), one finds that a total of $3,000 worth of output was created.

Another—and far simpler—way to avoid the over-counting problem is to focus exclusively on final sales, which implicitly account for the output created in all prior stages of production. Since consumers paid Company C, the retailer, $3,000 for the final tables and chairs, we can conclude that $3,000 worth of total output was created. Note that this was precisely the same answer we came to using the value-added approach in the previous paragraph. (See figure 1-1.)

Although both methods are correct, the second method—known as the expenditure method—has emerged as the standard approach for calculating GDP in most countries. The essential logic of the expenditure method is that if we add up all expenditures on *final* goods and services, then that sum must exactly equal the total value of national output produced, since every piece of output must eventually be purchased in one way or another.[1] As a result, *the standard definition of GDP is the market value of all final goods and services produced within a country over a given year.*

FIGURE 1-1

Calculating total output: an example

	Sales price	−	Cost of material inputs	=	Value added
Company A (forestry company) ↓	$1,000		$0		$1,000
Company B (furniture company) ↓	$2,500		$1,000		$1,500
Company C (retailer, to consumer)	$3,000		$2,500		$500
Total	$6,500		$3,500		$3,000

Government officials typically divide expenditure on final goods and services into five categories: consumption by households (C), investment in productive assets (I), government spending on goods and services (G), exports (EX), and imports (IM). One can find precise definitions for these categories in chapter 5.

The most important thing to remember, however, is that all of these categories are designed to avoid double counting. Although consumption includes almost *all* spending by households, business investment does not include all spending by firms. If it did, we would end up with massive double counting, because many of the things firms buy (such as raw materials) are ultimately processed and resold to consumers. As a result, investment only includes expenditures on output that is not expected to be used up in the short run (typically a year). For a carpenter, a new electric saw would represent investment, whereas the lumber that he buys to turn into tables and chairs would not.[2]

Another possible source of over-counting (in the expenditure method) involves imports. If American consumers bought televisions from Asia, we would have to be careful not to count those consumer expenditures in American GDP, since the output being purchased was foreign, not domestic. For this reason, imports are subtracted from total expenditures and thus appropriately excluded from GDP.

Putting these various pieces together yields one of the most important identities in macroeconomics:

$$\text{National Output (GDP)} = C + I + G + EX - IM.$$

This tells us that national output equals total expenditure on final goods and services, excluding imports. As we have seen, national output also equals the sum of value added (i.e., the incremental value added at every stage of production) throughout the domestic economy.

A third way to measure total output is to focus on income (though again, in practice, the expenditure method is used more often in calculating GDP). Income is the amount paid to factors of production, labor and capital, for their services—typically in the form of wages, salaries, interest, dividends, rent, and royalties. Since income is just payment for the production of output, it makes sense that total income should ultimately equal total output. After all, all of the proceeds of production ultimately have to end up somewhere, including in your pocket and mine.[3]

Exchange of Output Across Countries

Sometimes, one country may wish to exchange its output for that of another country. For example, the United States may wish to exchange commercial aircraft (such as Boeing 747s) for Japanese automobiles (such as Hondas or Toyotas). If the value of the U.S.

aircraft exactly equaled the value of the Japanese automobiles at the moment of exchange, then both countries' trade accounts would be in balance. That is, exports would exactly equal imports in both the United States and Japan.

One puzzle is why any country would want to run a trade surplus, which involves giving more of its output away to foreigners (in the form of exports) than it receives in return (in the form of imports). Why would any country wish to give away more than it received? The answer, in a nutshell, is that countries running trade surpluses today expect to get back additional output from their trading partners in the future.[4] This transfer across time is ensured through international lending and borrowing. When a country exports more than it imports, it inevitably lends an equivalent amount of funds abroad, which allows the foreigners to purchase its surplus production. Conversely, when a country imports more than it exports, it must borrow from foreigners to finance the difference. By borrowing, it is promising to pay back the difference—typically with interest—at some point in the future.

If, for instance, the United States were to import automobiles from Japan without exporting anything in return, it could pay for these automobiles only by borrowing from Japan. This borrowing could take many different forms: Americans could borrow directly from Japanese banks or they could give the Japanese stocks or bonds or other securities. Whatever form the borrowing took, the Japanese would end up with assets, such as stocks or bonds, promising a claim on future U.S. output. Eventually, when the Japanese decided to sell their American stocks and bonds and use the proceeds to buy American airplanes, movies, and software, the trade balances of the two countries would flip. Now the U.S. would be required to run a trade surplus, shipping some of its output to Japan, and thus forcing Americans to consume less than they produced. The Japanese, meanwhile, would now run a trade deficit, permitting their consumption to exceed their production (with the difference coming from the United States).

All international transactions of this sort are recorded in a country's balance of payments (BOP) statement. (See table 1-1.) Current transactions, such as exports and imports of goods and services, are recorded in the *current account*. Financial transactions, including sales of stocks and bonds to foreigners, are recorded in the *financial account* (which, until a few years ago, was called the capital account). Deficits on the current account are necessarily accompanied by capital inflows (borrowing) on the financial account, whereas surpluses on the current account are accompanied by capital outflows (lending) on the financial account. As a result, the current account and the financial account are perfect opposites, with a deficit in one necessarily accompanied by a surplus of the same amount in the other. (For pointers on reading a BOP statement, see chapter 6.)

Current account deficits should not necessarily be interpreted in a negative light, since they can indicate either weakness or strength, depending on the context. In some cases, current account deficits imply that a country is living beyond its means, increasing its consumption to an unsustainable level. But current account deficits can also arise when a country is borrowing from abroad in order to raise its level of domestic investment (and thus increase its future output). The question for deficit countries, therefore, is whether they are using the additional output well, whereas for surplus countries it is whether they can expect a good return in the future on the output they are giving to others today.

Although balance of payments accounting may be unfamiliar to you, it is not really as difficult as it may seem. In fact, the fundamental issues should become a good deal clearer through a

TABLE 1-1

GDP and the balance of payments—a hypothetical example (Country X)

GDP accounts for Country X, 2005 (millions of $)		Balance of payments for Country X, 2005 (millions of $)	
Consumption (C)	1,000	Current account	–50
Investment (I)	200	balance on merchandise	–200
Government (G)	300	balance on services	150
Exports (EX)	500	net investment income	–25
Imports (IM)	550	unilateral transfers	25
GDP (C + I + G + EX − IM)	**1,450**	Financial account	50
		net direct investment	–125
		net portfolio investment	150
		errors and omissions	–25
		change in official reserves	50

Explanation: In this example, Country X is buying more final output than it produces. We know this because C + I + G (domestic expenditure) is greater than total GDP (1,500 vs. 1,450). For this to be possible, Country X must import more than it exports, as is indeed the case. As shown in the left panel, imports (of goods and services) exceed exports (of goods and services) by 50, which is exactly the amount by which domestic expenditure exceeds domestic output. Clearly the difference between domestic expenditure and domestic output is being imported from abroad. The panel on the right side, the balance of payments, offers a more detailed account of Country X's transactions with the rest of the world. The current account is in deficit, reflecting the fact that Country X buys more from foreigners than it sells to foreigners. (Although the current account on the BOP does not always equal the difference between exports and imports as recorded in the GDP accounts, it is often close.) The surplus on the financial account represents a net capital inflow from abroad, which is necessary to finance the deficit on the current account. The capital inflows that make up the Financial Account take a variety of forms, including foreign direct investment (FDI), portfolio flows, and so on. For a more detailed treatment of GDP accounting and balance of payments accounting, see chapters 5 and 6.

simple analogy to your own personal budget. The amount of output that you produce—that is, your individual output—is reflected in your personal income. If you are employed, you are paid wages or a salary for your contribution to output. If you own capital (such as bank accounts, bonds, or stocks), you are paid interest or dividends for its contribution to output. If you wish to spend more than you produce (i.e., to buy more than your total income permits), then you have to borrow (or at least draw down your savings) to finance the difference. This excess spending may be used to finance increased consumption (such as a two-week holiday in Europe) or a new personal investment (such as additional education or an entrepreneurial venture) that promises to increase your earning power in the future. Either way, for you to borrow, someone else has to lend, which in turn means that that person is producing more than he or she is spending (and saving the difference so it can be lent to you). Someday you will have to repay the loan, presumably with interest. When you do that, you will have to consume less than you produce (i.e., consume less than your income would otherwise permit) because you will have to turn over part of your income to your creditor in the form of interest and principal repayments.

For a country, it is basically the same thing. If a nation is running a deficit on its current account (by importing more than it exports, for example), then it is using more output than it is producing, and it is borrowing the difference from foreigners, which registers as a surplus—a capital inflow—on the financial account of its BOP statement. The key point is that for a country, as for a person, the long-term constraint on consumption and investment is the amount of output that can be produced. A country, like a person, can use more output than it produces in the short run (by financing the difference through borrowing) but not over the long run. A nation's output—its GDP—thus represents its ultimate budget constraint, which is why the notion of national output lies at the heart of macroeconomics. (On the relationship between output and trade, see "A Brief Aside on the Theory of Comparative Advantage.")

A Brief Aside on the Theory of Comparative Advantage

One of the most important principles in all of economics is that of comparative advantage, first articulated by the British political economist David Ricardo in 1817. Intent on persuading British lawmakers to abandon their protectionist trade policies, Ricardo set out to prove the extraordinary power of trade to increase total world output and thus consumption and living standards. On the basis of a simple model with just two countries and two goods, he showed that every country—even one enjoying an absolute productivity advantage in both goods—would benefit from specializing in what it was relatively best at producing and then engaging in trade for everything else.

In his now-famous example, Ricardo imagined that Portugal was more productive than England in making both wine and cloth. Specifically, he assumed the Portuguese could produce, over a year, a particular quantity of wine (say, 8,000 gallons) with just 80 men, as compared to 120 men in England; and, similarly, that the Portuguese could produce a particular quantity of cloth (say, 9,000 yards) with just 90 men, as compared to 100 men in England. In other words, Portugal's productivity was 100 gallons of wine or 100 yards of cloth per worker per year, whereas England's was only 66.67 gallons of wine or 90 yards of cloth per worker per year. Given Portugal's absolute advantage in both industries, why would the Portuguese ever choose to buy either wine or cloth from England?

Ricardo's surprising answer was that both countries would benefit from trade, so long as both specialized in what they were *relatively* best at producing. In Ricardo's example, although Portugal was better at making both wine and cloth, its advantage was greater in wine. As a result, Portugal enjoyed a *comparative* advantage in wine, and, conversely, England enjoyed a *comparative* advantage in cloth. Ricardo concluded that if each country followed its comparative advantage—with Portugal producing only wine and England only cloth—and the two then engaged in trade with one another, each would be able to consume more wine *and* more cloth than if it had tried to produce both goods on its own.

To make this more concrete, assume that each country had 1,200 workers, and that each allocated 700 to wine and 500 to cloth. This would mean that Portugal produced 70,000 gallons of wine and 50,000 yards of cloth, whereas England produced 46,667 gallons of wine and 45,000 yards of cloth. However, if each country devoted all 1,200 workers to its comparative advantage, Portugal would produce 120,000 gallons of wine and England 108,000 yards of cloth. If they now traded, say, 48,000 gallons of wine for 55,000 yards of cloth, Portugal would end up with 72,000 gallons of wine and 55,000 yards of cloth, and England with 48,000 gallons of wine and 53,000 yards of cloth. Both countries, in other words, would end up with *more of both goods* as a result of specializing and trading. (See table 1-2.) In fact, to have produced these quantities on their own would have required 1,270 workers in Portugal and 1,309 workers in England. It is as if, as a result of specializing and trading according to the principle of comparative advantage, both countries got the output of many extra workers for free.

Economists have since shown that Ricardo's result can be generalized to as many countries and to as many goods as one wants to include. Although we can certainly specify conditions under which mutual gains from trade break down, most economists tend to believe that these conditions—these possible exceptions

---

TABLE 1-2

Comparative advantage and gains from trade: a numeric example

	Wine (gallons)	Cloth (yards)
Portuguese productivity (output per worker per year)	100	100
English productivity (output per worker per year)	66.67	90
Ratio of Portuguese productivity to English productivity	1.5 (Portuguese comparative average)	1.1 (English comparative average)
Portuguese output under autarchy (700 wine workers, 500 cloth workers)	70,000	50,000
English output under autarchy (700 wine workers, 500 cloth workers)	46,667	45,000
Portuguese output under specialization (1,200 wine workers)	120,000	0
English output under specialization (1,200 cloth workers)	0	108,000
Portuguese consumption after trade (e.g., 48,000 gallons of wine for 55,000 yards of cloth	72,000	55,000
English consumption after trade (e.g., 55,000 yards of cloth for 48,000 gallons of wine)	48,000	53,000

---

to free trade—occur relatively rarely in practice. Indeed, the Nobel Prize-winning economist Paul Samuelson once acknowledged that "it is a simplified theory. Yet, for all its oversimplification, the theory of comparative advantage provides a most important glimpse of truth. Political economy has found few more pregnant principles. A nation that neglects comparative advantage may pay a heavy price in terms of living standards and growth."

Remarkably, most of us—even those who have never studied the theory of comparative advantage—tend to live by it in our own personal affairs every day. For the most part, we all try to do what we're relatively best at and trade for everything else. Take an investment banker, for example. Even if that investment banker were better at painting houses than any professional painter in town, she would still probably be wise (from an economic standpoint) to focus on investment banking and to pay others to paint her house for her, rather than to paint it herself. This is because her *comparative* advantage is presumably in investment banking, not house painting. Taking time away from her high-paying investment banking job in order to paint her house would likely prove quite costly, ultimately reducing the amount of money she could earn and, in turn, the amount of output she could consume. In order to maximize output, in other words, it makes sense for each of us to specialize in our comparative advantage and to trade for the rest.

What Makes Output Go Up and Down?

Many macroeconomists regard the question of what makes national output go up and down as the most important question of all. Although there is remarkably little agreement on the answer, there are at least a few things on which most economists do agree.

Sources of Growth

Beginning with the question of what makes output rise over time, economists often point to three basic sources of economic growth: increases in labor, increases in capital, and increases in the efficiency with which these two factors are used. The amount of labor can rise if existing workers work longer hours or if the workforce is expanded through new entrants (such as occurred in the United States in the 1970s, when previously nonemployed women began entering the paid workforce in large numbers). Capital stock rises when businesses enhance their productive capacity by adding more plant and equipment (through investment). Efficiency increases when producers are able to get more output from the same amount of labor and capital—as a result of organizational innovation, for example.

As an illustration of these different sources of growth, consider a simple textile factory with ten employees and ten sewing machines. If each employee, making whole shirts on a sewing machine, were able to produce ten shirts per day, then the total output of the factory would be 100 shirts per day. Now imagine that the factory owner doubled both the number of workers and the number of sewing machines. Output would undoubtedly rise—perhaps to 200 shirts per day. Thus, one strategy for increasing output is to increase labor, capital, or a combination of the two. A very different strategy, however, would aim for an increase in efficiency, rather than labor and capital inputs. The factory owner, for example, might try to enhance efficiency by reorganizing the shop floor, setting up something resembling an assembly line. Under the new arrangement, instead of each worker making whole shirts, some workers would make collars, others sleeves, and so on. Workers at the end of the line would assemble the various pieces. If this approach were substantially more efficient, the factory—with its original ten workers and ten sewing machines—might now be able to produce as many as 200 shirts per day, or more, even with no increase in labor or capital.[5] Economists often refer to such efficiency as total factor productivity (or TFP). (For further discussion of TFP, see "Productivity.")

Productivity

A lthough total factor productivity is an important macroeconomic concept, it is not typically what economists and other analysts have in mind when they refer simply to "productivity." Instead, the word is commonly used as a shorthand for labor productivity, defined as output per worker hour (or, in some cases, as output per worker). If you read in the newspaper that hourly productivity increased by 3 percent last year, this means that real GDP (output) divided by the total number of hours worked nationwide was 3 percent higher at the end of last year than it was at the end of the previous year. In general, countries with high labor productivity enjoy higher wages and living standards than countries with low labor productivity.

There are many reasons why labor productivity might be higher in one country than another, or why it might grow in a given country from one year to the next. In particular, greater availability of machinery and other capital equipment is typically associated with higher labor productivity. As one economist has noted, "Railroad workers, on average, can each move more tons of freight than the average bicyclist."[a] Better educated workers also tend to be more productive than their less educated counterparts, with college-educated workers generally producing more output per hour (and earning higher wages) than high-school-educated workers.

Economic analysts often pay close attention to the relationship between productivity and wages. When a country's wages are rising faster than its labor productivity, economists say that its unit labor costs (i.e., the cost of labor needed to produce a unit of output) are rising. When, conversely, increases in labor productivity outpace increases in wages, unit labor costs are said to be falling. Countries whose unit labor costs (as measured in a common currency) are rising faster than those of their trade partners are often said to be "losing competitiveness" in the global marketplace.

[a] Forest Reinhardt, "Accounting for Productivity Growth," Case No. 794-051 (Boston: Harvard Business School, Sept. 14, 1994): 3. When labor productivity rises by more than one would expect from an increase in the capital stock alone, economists attribute the difference to *total factor productivity*, which broadly measures the efficiency with which labor and capital are used.

Although the illustration just given involved but a single factory, the same basic principles can be applied to entire economies. A national economy may increase its GDP by increasing the total number of person-hours worked (labor), by increasing the total amount of plant and equipment in use (capital), or by increasing the efficiency with which labor and capital are used (TFP).

So-called supply-side economists focus their attention on how to grow all three of these factors, in order to increase the total potential output—the supply side—of an economy. One favorite method among "supply-siders" in the United States is the reduction of tax rates. Supply-side economists argue that because lower tax rates allow everyone in the private sector to keep more of what they earn, tax relief provides citizens with strong incentives to work longer hours (thus increasing labor), to save and invest more of their income (thus increasing capital), and to devote more attention to innovation of all kinds (thus increasing efficiency, or TFP). For all of these reasons, supply-siders in the

United States have often favored reductions in tax rates as the best way to grow GDP over the long run.

Other economists, including many outside of the United States, have at times argued almost exactly the opposite—that *government-led* investment (in public infrastructure, education, and R&D, for example) can be the best way to build the capital stock, enhance the labor force, and promote innovation and thus the best way to boost long-run economic growth. Although they, too, focus on the supply side, they have a very different conception of the optimal use of public policy in boosting potential output (supply).

Causes of Economic Downturns
(Recessions and Depressions)

Another question of great importance among macroeconomists is what makes output decline or grow more slowly. Clearly, anything that causes labor, capital, or TFP to fall could potentially cause a decline in output, or at least a decline in its rate of growth. A massive earthquake, for example, could reduce output by destroying vast amounts of physical capital. Similarly, a deadly epidemic could reduce output by decimating the labor force. Even something as seemingly noneconomic as religious strife could reduce output, by increasing tensions among employees of different faiths and thus reducing their collective efficiency and, in turn, TFP.

In some cases, however, output may decline sharply even in the absence of any earthquakes or epidemics. From 1929 to 1933, for example, national output declined by more than 30 percent in the United States. Economists and policy makers alike were as puzzled as they were horrified. President Herbert Hoover observed in October 1930 that although the economy was in a depression, "the fundamental assets of the Nation . . .

have been unimpaired. . . . The gigantic equipment and unparalleled organization for production and distribution are in many parts even stronger than two years ago."[6] Similarly, in his inaugural address in early 1933, President Franklin Roosevelt maintained that "our distress comes from no failure of substance. We are stricken by no plague of locusts. . . . Plenty is at our doorstep, but a generous use of it languishes in the very sight of the supply."[7] Since all the necessary inputs (labor and capital) were there, why had output fallen so dramatically in just a few short years?

The British economist John Maynard Keynes claimed to have the answer. "If our poverty were due to earthquake or famine or war—if we lacked material things and the resources to produce them," he wrote in 1933, "we could not expect to find the means to prosperity except in hard work, abstinence, and invention. In fact, our predicament is notoriously of another kind. It comes from some failure in the immaterial devices of the mind. . . . Nothing is required, and nothing will avail, except a little clear thinking."[8] His key insight, implied by the phrase "immaterial devices of the mind," was that the problem was mainly one of expectations and psychology. For some reason, people had gotten it into their heads that the economy was in trouble, and that belief rapidly became self-fulfilling. Families decided that they had better save more to prepare for the future. Seeing a drop in consumption on the horizon, businesses decided to scale back both investment and production, leading to layoffs, which reduced workers' incomes and thus exacerbated the drop in consumption.

Driven by nothing more than expectations, which Keynes would later refer to as "animal spirits," the economy had fallen into a vicious downward spiral. Although the economy's *potential* output remained large (since all the same factories were still there and the same workers still available, if called upon), *actual* output had collapsed as a result of a severe shortfall in demand.

In principle, such a collapse could not have occurred had prices been perfectly flexible and adjusted instantly to reequilibrate supply and demand. For example, if wages had fallen fast enough (and far enough) to reflect a reduced demand for labor, all unemployed workers would quickly have found new jobs, though admittedly at lower wages than they had enjoyed before. The point is that even with sudden changes in expectations, resources would never go to waste—or remain unemployed—if the price mechanism worked perfectly.

In practice, however, markets sometimes falter. For reasons that are still not fully understood, prices can be rigid or sticky, meaning that they don't always adjust as quickly or as completely as they should. As a result, a negative shock—including a sudden downturn in expectations—truly can drive an economy into an extended recession, where real incomes decline and both human and physical resources are left unemployed.

Starting around the time of Keynes, therefore, economists began to realize that there was more to economic growth than just the supply side. Demand mattered a great deal as well, particularly since it could sometimes fall short. In fact, over roughly the next 40 years, it became an article of faith among leading economists and government officials that it was the government's responsibility to "manage demand" through fiscal and monetary policy, so as to reduce the duration and the severity of economic recessions and thus help stabilize the business cycle.* (Figure 1-2 charts the U.S. business cycle.)

---

* Economists commonly distinguish between long-term (secular) trends and short-term (cyclical) fluctuations. Recessions, which tend to come and go, are generally regarded as cyclical phenomena. Although there is no universally accepted definition of a recession, one rule of thumb is that a recession involves at least two consecutive quarters of negative real GDP growth.

FIGURE 1-2

The U.S. business cycle, 1930–2005

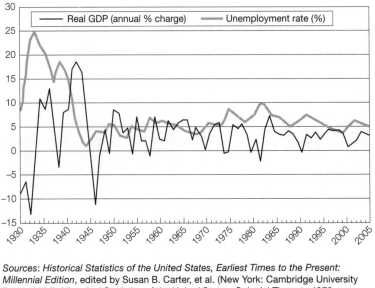

Sources: *Historical Statistics of the United States, Earliest Times to the Present: Millennial Edition*, edited by Susan B. Carter, et al. (New York: Cambridge University Press, 2006); *Historical Statistics of the United States: Colonial Times to 1970* (Washington, DC: GPO, 1975); U.S. Bureau of Labor Statistics; U.S. Bureau of Economic Analysis.

We will return to these topics in greater detail in chapter 3. But for now it is worth remembering that *actual* output can fall short of *potential* output when demand falters. Labor, capital, and TFP are all very important, but so too are expectations.

Isn't Wealth More Important Than Output?

With all this focus on output, even a loyal reader may be starting to entertain some doubts. One might be wondering, for instance, whether wealth isn't more important than output in determining a nation's well being. Although this is a very good question, the answer, in a word, is "no."

Unquestionably, people feel rich when they own lots of financial assets, such as stocks and bonds. But the reason they feel rich is that these assets provide them, indirectly, with a claim on future output. If they own stock in a company, for example, then they are entitled to a share of its future profits, which are in turn based on the output the company produces and sells. Another way to look at this is that people who own lots of financial assets feel rich because they believe they can always sell the assets for money and use the proceeds to buy any goods and services their hearts desire. In this sense as well, wealth simply represents a claim on future output.[9] Clearly, if the production of output collapsed and there were few goods or services to buy (because of a massive epidemic, for example), then most assets—including stocks and bonds—would quickly lose much of their value, with some even becoming worthless. Indeed, this is why financial assets typically lose value in a depression, when output falls.

At root, most *financial* assets represent claims on real productive assets (such as plant and equipment), which in turn are expected to generate output in the future. But of course, all of these productive assets were once output themselves. One of the most important decisions that a society has to make—at least implicitly—is what to do with the output it produces. One option is simply to consume all of it every year. The problem with focusing solely on the present is that it may eliminate the chance for a brighter future. Instead of consuming everything today, a better strategy might be to save something for tomorrow. In fact, it might be possible to produce far more output in the future if some fraction of today's resources were used to make productive assets (such as the sewing machines needed to make clothes) rather than just consumables (such as the clothes themselves).

Current output that is intended to increase future output is called investment. Fundamentally, investment can be financed in one of two ways—either through domestic savings (which implies reduced consumption today) or through borrowing from abroad (which implies reduced consumption tomorrow). In the United States at the present time, Americans do some of both. (See figure 1-3.)

FIGURE 1-3

Domestic expenditure, domestic output, and sources of investment in the United States, 2005

Domestic expenditure (uses of output)	Share of GDP (%)
Private and government consumption	86
Private and government investment	20
Total	106
Sources of investment	
Domestic savings	13
Net borrowing from abroad	6
Statistical discrepancy	1
Total	20
Expenditure versus output	
Total domestic expenditure	106
Total domestic output (GDP)	100
Difference (= net borrowing from abroad)	6

Source: Bureau of Economic Analysis, U.S. Department of Commerce

Note: In the U.S. in 2005, domestic expenditures (uses of output) exceeded domestic production of output (GDP) by about 6%. Similarly, total domestic investment exceeded total domestic savings—again by about 6% (20% investment minus 13% savings minus 1% statistical discrepancy). In both cases, the difference was made up by "borrowing" 6% of output from abroad (as expressed in the current account deficit).

In a market economy, decision making about savings and investment is highly decentralized. Based on expected returns and the cost of borrowing, as well as their own preferences, households decide how much to save, firms decide how much to invest, and foreigners decide how much to lend. In some cases, the government may try to influence the result—by offering, for example, an investment tax credit or other incentives to encourage additional business expenditure on plant and equipment. For the most part, however, these critical decisions are made privately in the marketplace every single day, by households, firms, and foreign investors.

Ultimately, the output the market allocates to investment (rather than to consumption) adds to the nation's capital stock. There is no question that capital is vital in a *capitalist* economy. Hence the name. But it is equally important to remember that capital is derived from output and, ultimately, that it is but a means to an end—the end being to produce (and to have access to) more output in the future. Indeed, a nation is generally classified as rich or poor depending on its output per person (GDP per capita), with the United States near the top of the list ($42,024 GDP per capita in 2005) and Burundi ($107) and Ethiopia ($126) near the bottom.[10] (For more on the relationship between saving, investment, and output, see "The Pension Dilemma and the Centrality of Output".)

The Pension Dilemma and the Centrality of Output

As is well known, many nations' pay-as-you-go pension systems are expected to run into trouble in the coming years. Once the baby boomers begin to retire, each active worker paying into a national pension system will have to support an ever-larger number of retirees.

Although the debate over pension reform has become highly contentious (and highly technical) in many countries, the essential problem is really quite simple, and it boils down to output. Each year, there is only so much national output to go around, and it somehow has to be divided between active workers (who produce it) and a growing number of retirees (who mainly just consume it). This, at root, is the job of a pension system—to divide national output between active workers and retirees. Keeping this simple point in mind is helpful in thinking about the basic challenges ahead and about the tradeoffs involved in various reform proposals.

One proposed reform envisions the creation of new government-sponsored individual retirement accounts (IRAs). Whereas a pay-as-you-go pension system offers retirees an implicit claim on labor (since benefits are generally financed through a payroll tax on employment), a system based on IRAs would offer retirees a claim on capital (as represented by the stocks and bonds they held in their accounts). In other words, the pay-as-you-go approach and the IRA approach simply offer two different ways to divide the pie.

Unfortunately, some proponents of the IRA approach suggest that there is a "free lunch" to be had: if only Americans could use their Social Security contributions to buy stocks and bonds, rather than to pay for the benefits of current retirees, they could build nice nest eggs and comfortably retire without being a drain on anyone. Current benefits, meanwhile, could be financed through borrowing until the transition was complete.

Not surprisingly, this free lunch argument rests on several fallacies. One basic mistake is to treat a portfolio of stocks and bonds as if it were a stockpile of actual output that an elderly person could consume straightaway. Although all of us are accustomed to thinking that we can sell our financial assets for cash at a moment's notice and then use the cash to buy goods and services, this obviously wouldn't work if everyone tried to do it at once. If a large number of senior citizens liquidated their financial assets at the same time, in order to buy needed goods and services, they would soon find that the proceeds were much smaller than they had expected. Simply giving the elderly more pieces of paper—more stocks and bonds—does not guarantee that there will be more output for them to consume in the future.

A related—but even more subtle—mistake is to view every contribution to an IRA as an addition to national savings, which would in turn raise national output in the future. The problem, once again, is that stocks and bonds are just pieces of paper. They represent legal claims on productive assets, but are not productive assets themselves. If every company in America decided to split its stock, doubling the number of shares in every American's portfolio, this would obviously not increase national savings. As we have seen, the only way to increase national savings at any moment in time is to reduce national consumption, and thus to devote more of the nation's precious output to investment in productive assets in order to raise output in the future. Whether or not IRAs would contribute to national savings depends entirely on how they were financed. If individuals or the government financed contributions to the new IRAs through borrowing, for example, then total savings would fail to rise as a result. To increase savings through the pension system, either current workers would have to put more of their income aside each year, or current retirees would have to accept lower benefits. Unfortunately, there's no free lunch.

The key question from a macroeconomic standpoint, therefore, is not whether the senior citizens of tomorrow have IRAs or traditional Social Security benefits, but whether they (or others) reduced their consumption to prepare for their eventual retirement. Unless savings are increased today, the division of output between active workers and retirees will be no less onerous tomorrow, regardless of whether we have a fully funded pension system based on individual accounts or a traditional pay-as-you-go system based on payroll taxes.

If this seems surprising—or even confusing—don't worry. The impending pension crisis is one of the toughest problems facing policy makers all around the world. But the underlying problem is more straightforward than it seems. The amount of output a country produces is its ultimate budget constraint, regardless of how many stocks or bonds or Social Security cards may be floating around. Unless its output grows, a country cannot give more to its retirees without giving less to its workers. The key point to remember is that as a society, it is mainly output, not wealth (and especially not financial wealth), that we have to rely on in the end.

CHAPTER TWO

Money

Although output is more important than wealth in the study of macroeconomics, one particular form of wealth—money—occupies a very special place in the field. Money serves many purposes in a market economy, but one of the most vital is to facilitate exchange. Without money, the exchange of goods and services would be far less efficient. As the British philosopher David Hume put it in the middle of the eighteenth century, money is not one "of the wheels of trade: It is the oil which renders the motion of the wheels more smooth and easy."[1]

Just imagine how complicated trade could become in the absence of money. If you were a farmer who grew wheat and wanted to take your family out to dinner, you would have to find a restaurant willing to accept a few bushels in exchange for a meal. Otherwise, you would have to figure out what the restaurant owner wanted—say, new chairs—and then find a furniture maker who was willing to trade chairs for wheat. And think what would happen if the furniture maker wasn't interested in wheat, but wanted a new hammer instead.

Clearly, having one convenient commodity that everyone was willing (or required) to accept as payment would simplify the process immensely. And this is precisely why money is used as a medium of exchange in every market economy around the world. In a monetized economy (where people transact with money), anyone wishing to purchase your wheat would simply pay money for it, allowing you to buy a meal at a restaurant or anything else you might want, subject solely to your having enough money to cover the cost.

At least since the dawn of the nation state, national governments have taken charge of defining what money is in their economies (see chapter 4). Eventually, almost every national government also took charge of creating its own currency, either by coining it or printing it itself. As we will see, how a government does this has enormous implications for how its economy functions and what types of risk its residents face in the marketplace.

Money and Its Effect on Interest Rates, Exchange Rates, and Inflation

Although money plays a vital role facilitating exchange, it also affects several variables that are of great interest to macroeconomists: interest rates, exchange rates, and the aggregate price level. In an important sense, all three of these variables constitute "prices" of money.

The interest rate can be thought of as the price of holding money or, alternatively, as the cost of investment funds. In general, most people would prefer to receive $100 in cash now than to receive the same $100 in cash a year from now. Economists characterize this trade-off as the "time value of money." A consumer may take out a loan (and agree to pay interest on it in the future) in order to receive cash to spend immediately. Perhaps this consumer prefers to start enjoying a new television set right away rather than saving up for a year before enjoying it. Similarly, business managers may wish to borrow from a bank or float bonds when the interest rate on borrowing is lower than the return they expect they can make on a new investment. When interest rates rise, money obviously becomes more expensive, both for individuals and for firms, and thus the cost of buying things today (relative to tomorrow or next year) goes up. In part for these reasons, rising interest rates tend to slow the growth of output in the economy (by slowing current consumption and investment), whereas falling interest rates tend to accelerate the growth of output (by stimulating current consumption and investment).

An exchange rate, meanwhile, is simply the price of one currency in terms of another. If it costs 100 yen to buy one dollar, then the yen-to-dollar exchange rate is 100. Conversely, the dollar-to-yen exchange rate is 0.01. If the yen-to-dollar exchange rate subsequently fell to 90, this would mean that the dollar had *depreciated* (and the yen had *appreciated*), since it now took more dollars to buy one yen (and fewer yen to buy one dollar).* When a country's exchange rate depreciates, foreigners will find

---

* It is important to note that when a country's exchange rate is expressed in terms of another currency (i.e., the other currency is in the denominator), an increase in the rate indicates depreciation of the country's currency, and a decrease indicates appreciation. For example, if the yen-to-dollar exchange rate "falls" from 100 to 90, then the Japanese yen has *appreciated* relative to the U.S. dollar, since it now takes fewer yen to buy one dollar (and, what is the same thing, one yen buys more dollars—or, in this case, a larger fraction of a dollar).

it cheaper to buy that country's currency, which may lead them to buy more of the country's goods as well. It is for this reason that a depreciating exchange rate is often regarded as being favorable for a country's exports. There is no free lunch, however. A depreciating exchange rate also means that foreign currencies (and thus foreign goods) appear more expensive to the country's citizens, thus reducing their overall purchasing power.

The aggregate price level (sometimes called the price deflator) is a bit more complicated, since it is not the price of any one thing in particular. Broadly speaking, the aggregate price level reflects the average price of *all* goods and services—or at least of a broad subset of goods and services—in terms of money. In a healthy economy, the money prices of individual goods and services are changing all the time. At any moment, some may be rising and others falling. Recently, for example, the price of milk was rising while the price of computers was falling. There are times, however, when one can detect trends across all (or at least most) prices. In a period of *inflation*, when the aggregate price level is increasing, most prices tend to rise, though some will inevitably rise more than others. In a period of *deflation*, by contrast, when the aggregate price level is decreasing, most prices tend to fall, though again some will fall more than others. It should not be hard to see that the value—or price—of money in terms of goods and services moves in exactly the opposite directions as the aggregate price level. When the price level rises (in a period of inflation), the value of money falls; and when the price level falls (in a period of deflation), the value of money rises. (See figure 2-1.)

As it turns out, changes in the *quantity* of money may affect all three of these variables—that is, all three "prices" of money. A nation's central bank can increase the money supply by printing

FIGURE 2-1

The three "prices" of money

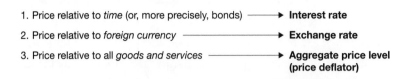

1. Price relative to *time* (or, more precisely, bonds) ——→ **Interest rate**
2. Price relative to *foreign currency* ———————→ **Exchange rate**
3. Price relative to all *goods and services* ———————→ **Aggregate price level (price deflator)**

more currency and injecting it into the economy. When the money supply rises, economists typically expect interest rates to fall. Although there is no clear consensus on exactly what drives interest rates, one way to think about this is that the price of a good tends to fall when its quantity increases. Just as the global price of oil tends to fall when more of it is pumped out of the Middle East, the price of obtaining money (the interest rate) tends to fall when the central bank injects more money into the domestic economy.

Similarly, when a country's money supply rises, economists generally expect the country's exchange rate to depreciate. Exchange rate determination, like interest rate determination, is an immensely difficult and controversial topic. So it is not possible to explore all of the various theories here. Once again, however, it is convenient simply to think in terms of supply and demand. Anything that affects the supply or demand for a currency will affect its exchange rate. If a new emphasis on quality in U.S. manufacturing were to make American goods more attractive all around the world, there would likely be an increased demand for U.S. dollars (since dollars are needed to buy American goods), and this would cause the dollar to appreciate. On the supply side, if the quantity of dollars in circulation were to rise relative to other currencies, then its price in terms of the other currencies would likely fall (depreciate). (For a more detailed treatment of exchange rates, see chapter 7.)

This brings us to the third variable—the aggregate price level—and its relationship to money. Economists generally regard an increase in the money supply—and particularly large increases in the money supply—as inflationary. Money growth, in other words, tends to drive up the price level. With more cash in their pockets and bank accounts, consumers often find new reasons to buy things. But unless the supply of goods and services has increased in the meantime, the consumers' mounting demand for products will simply bid up prices, thus stoking inflation. Economists sometimes say that inflation rises when "too much money is chasing too few goods."

Individually, each of these causal relationships is fairly clear. Each is also symmetric: whereas an *increase* in the money supply tends to depress the interest rate, depreciate the exchange rate, and increase the price level, a *decrease* in the money supply tends to lift the interest rate, appreciate the exchange rate, and decrease the price level. (See figure 2-2.)

FIGURE 2-2

Money: standard "textbook" relationships

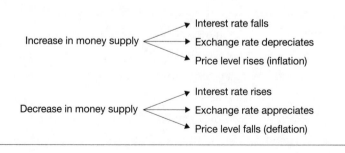

Nominal Versus Real

These relationships between money and other macroeconomic variables become somewhat complex when the variables begin to interact. A good example involves the interaction of interest rates and inflation. Although an increase in the money supply is expected to drive down interest rates, it is also expected to drive up inflation, which may in turn push long-term interest rates (and, eventually, short-term rates) *higher*, rather than lower. To understand why, it is first necessary to understand one of the central dichotomies in macroeconomics: nominal versus real.

Nominal Versus Real GDP

We'll start with nominal versus real GDP. During an inflationary period, when all prices are generally on an upward trend, GDP may rise even if no additional goods and services are being produced. This is because GDP is measured in terms of *current* (market) prices. Recall that in calculating GDP, officials add up the value of all final goods and services produced in an economy in a given year, and they value these goods based on the prices at which they are sold.

As an illustration, suppose that an island economy produced only two final goods, coconut milk and rice. Imagine further that in the year 2005, it produced 1 million gallons of coconut milk, which it sold at $10 per gallon, and 2 million pounds of rice, which it sold at $4 per pound. Just a little bit of calculation reveals that the island's GDP in 2005 was $18 million. (See table 2-1.) Now suppose that for some reason the island still produced 1 million gallons of coconut milk and 2 million pounds of rice in

TABLE 2-1

Final output of island economy, 2005 (in current island $)

Output	Quantity	Price	Value of final output
Coconut milk	1 million gallons	$10/gallon	$10 million
Rice	2 million pounds	$4/pound	$8 million
			$18 million (= 2005 GDP)

2006, but that the prices of these products on the island had doubled to $20 per gallon and $8 per pound, respectively. Naturally, the country's GDP would rise to $36 million in 2006, though its actual output (i.e., gallons of coconut milk and pounds of rice produced) had not increased at all. (See table 2-2.) In this case, we would say that the island had experienced a 100 percent inflation rate (since prices had doubled), that its *nominal* GDP had also increased by 100 percent (having gone from $18 to $36 million), but that its *real* GDP (i.e., its GDP after controlling for inflation) had not changed.

Recall from the previous chapter that macroeconomists pay a great deal of attention to the quantity of goods and services an economy produces. This is because the more goods and services a nation produces (with a stable population), the higher the standard of living for those who live and work there. Whereas *nominal* GDP may increase either because of changes in *price* or changes in *quantity*, *real* GDP increases only with changes in *quantity*. Real GDP, in other words, measures the *quantity* of all final goods and services produced in a country in a given year. Another way of expressing this is in the following identity:

$$\text{Nominal GDP} = P \times Q,$$

where P is the aggregate price level (or price deflator) and Q is the total quantity of final output (real GDP).

TABLE 2-2

Final output of island economy, 2006 (in current island $)

Output	Quantity	Price	Value of final output
Coconut milk	1 million gallons	$20/gallon	$20 million
Rice	2 million pounds	$8/pound	$16 million
			$36 million (= 2006 GDP)

To reiterate, a country's prosperity depends on its real GDP (Q), not its nominal GDP (P × Q). As we saw in the island example, when nominal GDP rises solely because of price changes, residents are left no better off than they were before, since their command over real goods and services has not increased. Only when their access to goods and services rises—because of an increase in Q—are they truly better off in economic terms.

One way to calculate real GDP from year to year is to use a *constant* set of prices. In the island example, this would involve applying the prices in 2005 ($10 per gallon of coconut milk and $4 per pound of rice) to the output produced in both 2005 and 2006. Doing this would yield a real GDP of $18 million in 2005 and a real GDP of $18 million in 2006, accurately reflecting the fact that the quantity of output had not increased.

Naturally, the price deflator (P) can immediately be calculated for both 2005 and 2006, since we know both nominal and real GDP for both years. For any given year,

$$\text{Price deflator (P)} = \frac{\text{Nominal GDP}}{\text{Real GDP (Q)}}$$

This means that the price deflator (P) increased from 1.00 (i.e., $18 million/$18 million) in 2005 to 2.00 (i.e., $36 million/$18 million) in 2006, accurately reflecting the fact that prices doubled on the island from one year to the next.[2] (See table 2-3.)

TABLE 2-3

Island economy: nominal versus real GDP, 2005–2006

Year	Nominal GDP	=	Price deflator (P)	×	Real GDP (Q)
2005	$18 million		1.00		$18 million$_{2005\,\$}$
2006	$36 million		2.00		$18 million$_{2005\,\$}$

In a more typical example, we might see both nominal and real GDP rising, but nominal GDP rising faster. This would imply that national output was increasing, but that inflation was also present. In the United States between 1980 and 2000, for example, nominal GDP growth averaged 6.5 percent per year, while real GDP growth averaged 3.3 percent per year. The annual inflation rate (which will roughly equal the difference between nominal and real GDP growth) averaged 3.1 percent, meaning that prices were rising, on average, by 3.1 percent per year. (See table 2-4.) One way to characterize U.S. economic performance over

TABLE 2-4

United States economic performance, 1980–2000

	1980	2000	1980–2000 CAGR[a]
Nominal GDP ($P \times Q$)	$2,789.5 billion	$9,817.0 billion	6.5%
Real GDP, 2000 $ (Q)	$5,161.7 billion	$9,817.0 billion	3.3%
GDP deflator, 2000 = 100 (P)	54.0	100.0	3.1%

[a]CAGR stands for "compound annual growth rate." The formula for calculating a CAGR is as follows:

$$\text{CAGR} = [(\text{Final value/Starting value})^{[1/(\text{final year} - \text{starting year})]} - 1] \times 100\%$$

This formula is derived from the following growth equation:

$$\text{Final value} = \text{Starting value} \times (1 + r)^{(\text{number of years})},$$

where r is the average annual growth rate of the variable in question.

the 1980s and 1990s, therefore, is to say that slightly more than half of nominal GDP growth during these years was attributable to increases in quantity (real GDP) while the remainder was attributable to price increases (inflation). Had there been no inflation at all, nominal GDP growth and real GDP growth would have been exactly equal.

Nominal Versus Real Interest Rates

The same basic distinction—between nominal and real—can be applied to interest rates as well. A nominal interest rate is one that you find quoted at a bank or listed in the newspaper. If you borrowed $1,000 from a bank for one year at a nominal interest rate of 5 percent, at the end of that year you would owe the bank $1,050 (i.e., the original $1,000 in principal plus $1,000 × 5 percent, or $50, in interest). In 2005, the nominal interest rate on overnight bank lending in the United States (the so-called federal funds rate) averaged 3.22 percent, the nominal interest rate on 10-year U.S. government bonds 4.29 percent, and the nominal interest rate on 10-year home mortgages 5.94 percent. (The first of these, the overnight bank rate, is a short-term interest rate, whereas the second and third are long-term interest rates.)[3]

As already noted, nominal interest rates tend to rise with inflation. If a bank charged 5 percent interest on a loan when it anticipated zero inflation, it might charge 8 percent when it anticipated 3 percent inflation. In the latter scenario, the nominal rate would be 8 percent while the so-called *real interest rate* would remain at 5 percent. The approximate relationship between real and nominal interest rates can be expressed as follows:

$$\text{Real interest rate } (i_R) \approx \text{Nominal interest rate } (i_N)$$
$$- \text{ Expected inflation } (P^e)$$

Simply put, the real interest rate represents the effective rate of interest on a loan after controlling for inflation.

Nominal interest rates rise with inflation because creditors care about their command over real output, not their command over money per se. Imagine, for example, that a dairy farmer (let's call him Bill) agreed to lend his neighbor (Tom) ten milk cows for an entire season on the condition that Tom would return all ten plus one more cow at the end of the year. This would constitute a one-year loan at a 10 percent rate of interest. Now suppose that after repaying the loan at the end of the year (by delivering eleven cows to Bill), Tom wanted to do the same thing again—that is, he wanted to borrow ten cows from Bill for one year at a 10 percent rate of interest. The only difference was that this time he proposed repaying the loan in money rather than in cows. Since a cow cost $1,000 at the time of the agreement, Tom promised that he would pay Bill $11,000 at the end of the year. Bill thought this sounded fine and agreed to the deal. Unfortunately for Bill, however, the price of a cow increased by 10 percent that year, rising from $1,000 to $1,100. As a result, when Tom made good on the loan by paying Bill $11,000 at the end of the year, Bill was only able to buy ten cows, not eleven, with that sum of money. It was as if Bill had lent his original ten cows at no interest at all!

Economists would say that under the second arrangement, the *nominal* interest rate was 10 percent but that the *real* interest rate was zero. For Bill to have maintained an effective (*real*) rate of interest of 10 percent—that is, with regard to output rather than money—he would have had to raise his *nominal* interest rate to approximately 20 percent (or 21 percent, to be exact). At a 21 percent nominal rate of interest, Tom would have been required to repay $12,100 at the end of the year ($10,000 principal plus $2,100 interest), which would have been just enough to allow Bill to buy eleven cows at the new price of $1,100 each (since

11 × $1,100 = $12,100). It is easy to see from this example that if the price of cows had increased by one-tenth (i.e., if cow inflation were 10 percent), Bill would have had to roughly double the nominal rate of interest (in terms of money) to preserve a real rate of interest (in terms of cows) of 10 percent.

In assessing whether the cost of borrowing in an economy is high or low, economists typically focus on real rates rather than nominal rates. Once again, this is because output—not money— is what matters most.

Clearly, in a context of zero inflation, a 1,000 percent interest-rate loan would be very difficult to repay. If you borrowed $20,000 this year at 1,000 percent interest, you would have to repay $220,000 next year ($20,000 principal plus $200,000 interest). Since inflation was zero, both the real and nominal rate of interest would equal 1,000 percent. To consume an additional $20,000 worth of output this year, you would have to give up $220,000 worth of output the following year. By almost any standard, this would be very expensive credit.[4]

However, if inflation itself reached 1,000 percent, a nominal interest rate of 1,000 percent would no longer look burdensome for most borrowers—in fact, it would look very cheap—since wages and prices were rising by 1,000 percent as well. Under this second scenario, the nominal rate of interest would still be 1,000 percent, but the real rate of interest (i.e., nominal minus inflation) would have fallen to zero. As a result, borrowers lucky enough to get loans at 1,000 percent interest in an environment of 1,000 percent inflation would feel as if they were paying no interest at all, since—in terms of what it could actually buy—the $220,000 repayment would be no greater than the original $20,000 lent.[5] (See table 2-5.)

With all this in mind, we are now ready to reconsider why the relationship between money growth and interest rates can be

TABLE 2-5

Example: real versus nominal interest rates

	Nominal (posted) interest rate on loan	Rate of inflation	Real interest rate	Effective cost of borrowing
Scenario 1:	1,000%	0%	1,000%	Very high
Scenario 2:	1,000%	1,000%	0%	Very low

ambiguous. Normally, when the central bank increases the money supply, economists expect interest rates—especially short-term interest rates—to fall. However, growth in the money supply—particularly if it is substantial—may also spark inflationary expectations, which in turn will tend to push long-term nominal interest rates upward. And if inflation indeed takes hold, short-term nominal interest rates will eventually rise as well. Because of these conflicting pressures (one pushing down and the other pushing up), the ultimate effect on nominal interest rates of a large increase in money supply is ambiguous. Real interest rates are very likely to fall. Short-term nominal rates will almost surely fall immediately, but may rise later on if inflation kicks in. And long-term nominal rates may fall, rise, or stay the same, depending mainly on what happens to inflationary expectations. (See figure 2-3.)

FIGURE 2-3

Money growth, inflation, and interest rates (nominal versus real)

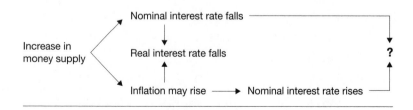

Nominal Versus Real Exchange Rates

The distinction between nominal and real can be applied to exchange rates as well. Even if a country's nominal exchange rate is depreciating, its real exchange rate will depreciate less (or may even appreciate) if inflation is rising faster than in other countries.

To understand why, we should start with nominal exchange rates. As we have seen, if a country's currency depreciates relative to other currencies, then it will appear cheaper to foreigners. This, in turn, will make the country's goods and services look cheaper to foreigners, which may well entice them to buy more of the country's exports. The country's own citizens, meanwhile, will find it more expensive to buy foreign currencies, which may deter them from buying as many imports from abroad. It is in this sense that depreciation of a country's currency is seen as favorable to its trade balance (since its exports will tend to rise and its imports will tend to fall).

A simple illustration should help make this clear. Imagine that the yen-to-dollar exchange rate was 100 (i.e., 100 yen to 1 dollar) and that a Japanese-made calculator cost ¥900 in Japan and an American-made calculator cost $10 in the United States. If transportation costs were low, Americans would prefer to import Japanese-made calculators, since they would cost only $9 at the prevailing exchange rate (plus a bit more for transportation), as compared to $10 for American-made calculators. Now suppose that the dollar depreciated by 20 percent, driving the yen-to-dollar exchange rate to 80. If the price of domestically produced calculators didn't change in either country, Americans would start buying American calculators, since Japanese calculators would now cost $11.25 (i.e., 900/80) plus transportation costs, while American calculators would still cost $10. Simultaneously,

Japanese might now prefer American-made calculators as well, since they would cost only ¥800 at the new exchange rate (plus transportation costs), as compared to ¥900 for Japanese-made calculators. Thus, after its currency depreciated, America's imports would fall and its exports would rise. (See table 2-6.)

This result could be completely negated, however, if the United States experienced rising inflation at the same time. Suppose, as in the previous example, the U.S. dollar depreciated by 20 percent (to a yen-to-dollar exchange rate of 80), but that this time the United States experienced 30 percent inflation, while Japan experienced no inflation at all. Because of the rise in American inflation, the price of an American-made calculator would likely rise by 30 percent to $13 or ¥1,040 (at the exchange rate of 80 yen to the dollar). Since Japanese calculators would still cost only ¥900 or $11.25 (at the exchange rate of 80 yen to the dollar), both Japanese and Americans would likely revert to buying Japanese-made calculators. American imports would rise, and American exports would fall—just as if its currency had *appreciated*. In fact, although its *nominal* exchange rate had *depreciated* by 20 percent, its *real exchange rate* (i.e., the effective exchange rate after controlling for inflation) had actually *appreci-*

TABLE 2-6

Cost of calculators, in $ and ¥, before and after nominal depreciation of the dollar

	¥/$ ER	Cost of U.S.-made calculator ($)	Cost of U.S.-made calculator (¥)	Cost of Japanese-made calculator (¥)	Cost of Japanese-made calculator ($)	Country from which calculators bought
Before	100	$10	¥1,000	¥900	$9.00	Japan
After	80	$10	¥800	¥900	$11.25	U.S.

ated, because its inflation rate (relative to Japan's) had increased by *more* than 20 percent.

The relationship between real and nominal exchange rates in this example can be expressed in the following approximation (which obviously can be applied to any two countries, not just the United States and Japan):

$$\%\Delta\text{Real exchange rate (¥/\$)}$$
$$\approx \%\Delta\text{Nominal exchange rate (¥/\$)}$$
$$- (\text{Japanese inflation } \% - \text{U.S. inflation } \%)$$

If we assume, for convenience, that foreign inflation is zero, then (by rearranging terms) we can also say that the real appreciation of a country's currency approximately equals the country's inflation rate minus its nominal depreciation rate—that is:

$$\text{Real appreciation of Currency X}$$
$$\approx \text{Inflation rate of Country X}$$
$$- \text{Nominal depreciation of Currency X}$$

where all of these changes are expressed in percentages. (See table 2-7.)

Although the notion of a *real* exchange rate remains unfamiliar to many business managers and investors, those involved in international transactions ignore it at their peril. Consider just one example. In the early 1990s, as U.S. investment was pouring into Mexico, many American portfolio managers celebrated Mexico's pegged nominal exchange rate as an important safeguard of their investments.[6] But they seemed to pay scant attention to Mexico's rapidly appreciating real exchange rate, which resulted from the combination of its pegged nominal rate against the dollar on the

TABLE 2-7

Nominal versus real exchange rates—four scenarios

	% change in **nominal** ¥/$ exchange rate	Inflation rate (Japan)	Inflation rate (U.S.)	Approx % change in **real** ¥/$ exchange rate	Expected effect on U.S. balance of trade
Scenario 1:	–20% (depreciation of $)	0%	30%	10% (appreciation of $)	Unfavorable (↓ BOT)
Scenario 2:	–20% (depreciation of $)	0%	20%	0%	Neutral
Scenario 3:	–20% (depreciation of $)	0%	10%	–10% (depreciation of $)	Favorable (↑ BOT)
Scenario 4:	–20% (depreciation of $)	30%	30%	–20% (depreciation of $)	Favorable (↑ BOT)

one hand and inflation that was running higher than inflation in the United States on the other. To be sure, the peso's dramatic real appreciation offered an important signal of potential trouble ahead, undermining Mexico's trade position and thus intensifying its dependence on ever-larger inflows of foreign capital. Particularly well-informed investors may have recognized that a large real appreciation could presage a substantial depreciation of the nominal exchange rate (and thus a sharp decline in the dollar value of their peso-denominated assets). Most investors, however, were apparently caught by surprise—and suffered big losses—when the peso collapsed in a full-blown currency crisis beginning in late 1994. Clearly, the concept of a real exchange rate, though rather academic-sounding, can be of profound practical significance in business transactions. (See "Real Exchange Rates and Foreign Investment.")

We return to exchange rates in subsequent sections (and in chapter 7). But for now, it is worth noting how the nominal–real divide can affect the relationship between money growth, exchange rates, and the balance of trade. As already suggested, substantial money growth in a country is likely to cause the country's *nominal* exchange rate to *depreciate*. But substantial money growth can also spark domestic inflation, which can cause the *real* exchange rate to move in the other direction. The key question is whether domestic inflation is greater than exchange-rate depreciation—or, more precisely, whether the difference between domestic and foreign inflation is larger than the depreciation of the domestic currency relative to the foreign currency. If the inflation-rate differential (domestic minus foreign) exceeds the nominal rate of depreciation of the exchange rate, then the real exchange rate will appreciate, placing downward pressure on the balance of trade. If the inflation-rate differential is less than the

Real Exchange Rates and Foreign Investment

A basic understanding of real exchange rates (and how they affect company sales and profits) is vital for any business manager engaged in international trade or investment.

Consider, for example, a manager responsible for the Chinese production subsidiary of an American mobile phone company. Because China (like many developing countries) essentially pegs its exchange rate to the dollar, the manager would be wise to think hard about the implications of a sudden surge in Chinese inflation. After all, if prices rose faster in China than in the United States, then the yuan would appreciate in *real* terms against the dollar, even though the nominal exchange rate (that is, the one reported in the newspaper and on the Web) remained steady as a rock, held in place by an official exchange-rate peg.

This real appreciation of the yuan would generate three (potentially conflicting) effects on the subsidiary in China:

1. More intense price competition from foreign imports into the Chinese market

2. More intense price competition from foreign producers within foreign markets; and

3. A more favorable effective rate of repatriation on profit margins earned within China

Clearly, the first two effects would be quite negative for the subsidiary, while the third would be positive, so long as there were still some profits left to repatriate.

The reason that price competition would become stiffer for the American subsidiary operating in China is that it would face higher production costs (including higher wages and higher domestic input prices) as a consequence of rising Chinese inflation. If the subsidiary tried to pass these higher costs along to consumers in the form of higher prices, then it would risk losing market share—both in and outside of China—to American (and other foreign) producers that didn't face comparable cost increases at home.

Confronted with a *real* appreciation of the yuan, the subsidiary's manager would thus face the unenviable choice of either squeezing margins to protect market share or surrendering market share to maintain margins. Either way, it would be bad news for the subsidiary's bottom line.

In fact, the only possible good news would involve repatriation. If the subsidiary had enjoyed, say, a 10 percent margin on sales before the real appreciation, and if it somehow managed to preserve this margin afterward (a rather big *if*, to be sure), the same 10 percent margin would now—because of Chinese inflation—translate into a larger number of nominal yuan. And, with the nominal exchange rate still pegged to the dollar (at the same official rate), a larger number of yuan would inevitably translate into a larger number of dollars, once repatriated.

The point is that the effects of a *real* appreciation, triggered by inflation, will closely mimic the effects of a nominal appreciation, both favorable and unfavorable, even though the nominal exchange rate hasn't budged. Unfortunately, many business managers—particularly those with little experience in international markets—remain far more alert to changes in nominal exchange rates than to changes in real exchange rates, even though the latter may be every bit as important in determining the health and vitality of their firms.

FIGURE 2-4

Money growth, inflation, and exchange rates (nominal versus real)

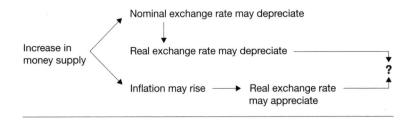

nominal rate of depreciation of the exchange rate, then the real exchange rate will depreciate, placing upward pressure on the balance of trade. (See figure 2-4.)

Money Illusion and Sticky Wages

In an ideal world, individuals would always be able to distinguish real economic changes from merely nominal ones. If a worker's wage rose by exactly the same percentage as the overall price level, she would recognize that her purchasing power had not increased as a result. Even though her monthly payroll checks would look larger in *nominal* terms, she would still not be able to buy more goods and services than before because the prices of those goods would have increased exactly in proportion to her pay, thus leaving her *real* wage unchanged.

Although in principle this distinction should be clear, in practice it can be murky. One potential problem, which remains controversial among economists, is the notion that many individuals suffer from "money illusion." That is, they may sometimes appear to be more concerned about nominal values rather than real values. Workers, for example, may worry more about the size of their *nominal* wage than about their *real* purchasing power. If true, money illusion could help to explain why nominal wages tend to be sticky, particularly on the downside. When prices rise, workers may fail to demand sufficient wage increases to prevent the inflation from cutting into their purchasing power. However, when prices fall, these same workers may—if influenced by money illusion—fiercely oppose any suggestion of nominal wage reductions, even though their real purchasing power has grown dramatically as a result of the deflation.

Some economists view wage stickiness as a cause of unemployment during periods of deflation (falling prices). If workers refused to accept smaller nominal wages during such periods (potentially as a result of money illusion), their *real* wages would rise rapidly as prices fell. Eventually, their real wages would reach a level that their employers simply could no longer afford to pay, and the workers would be laid off. If only the workers had focused on maintaining their *real* wages rather than their *nominal* wages, the argument goes, they might have kept their jobs.

The notion of money illusion dates back a long way. In fact, the American economist Irving Fisher published a seminal book on the subject in 1928.[7] Although few economists today regard money illusion as a major source of wage rigidity, it nonetheless stands out as an early—if now contested—explanation for why wages may not always adjust as rapidly in practice as they should in theory.

Money and Banking

So far, we have talked quite a bit about money without saying much about where it comes from or about the different forms it takes.

In most countries, only the government can issue currency, which is "legal tender" and therefore required by law to be accepted as payment for all debts. Take a look at a dollar bill and note what is imprinted on the front: "This note is legal tender for all debts, public and private." Currency thus serves as a very reliable and convenient means of payment for many transactions. Typically, national central banks take responsibility for deciding how much currency to issue. In the United States, the central bank is called the Federal Reserve. If you take another look at that dollar bill, you will notice the words "Federal Reserve Note" printed at the very top, indicating that the bill is an obligation of the Federal Reserve.[8]

Although the central bank decides how much currency to issue, it is important to recognize that the central bank is not the only institution that creates money. Commercial banks play a crucial role as well. This is because currency is not the only form of money. According to a standard definition of the money supply known as M1, checking accounts also count as money since checks are widely accepted as a means of payment and are highly liquid—that is, they can easily be converted to currency.

Because checking accounts allow the account holders either to withdraw or to transfer the deposited funds on demand, economists typically refer to these accounts as "demand deposits." And demand deposits are an important component of the money supply. At the end of 2005 there was a total of $724 billion worth of U.S. currency (i.e., one-dollar bills, five-dollar bills, ten-dollar bills, and so forth) in circulation. At the same time, banks and thrifts held a total of $638 billion in demand (and other checkable) deposits. As just noted, M1 money supply includes these two items: currency in circulation and demand deposits, both of which are widely used—and widely accepted—as means of payment.[9]

Because checking accounts constitute an important form of money, commercial banks play a vital role in money creation. Through a process of taking deposits and lending out most of the funds received, banks actually expand the money supply beyond the amount of currency in circulation.

Imagine, for example, that you go to the bank and deposit $100 in cash into your checking account. At that moment, the size of the overall money supply doesn't change. You have an additional $100 in your checking account, but the $100 you once had in your pocket is now in a bank vault. Because the cash is no longer in circulation, it is not included in M1 money supply. However, in most cases, the bank will quickly lend out most of that cash, limited only by a legal reserve requirement (which compels the bank to keep about 10 percent of the cash on reserve). Now the money supply *has* increased. You have your $100 in the form of a demand deposit (checking account), and the person who borrowed from the bank has, say, $90 of the cash that you used to have in your pocket. So the money supply has increased by $90. As you may have guessed, however, the process doesn't end there. If the borrower buys something with that cash and the recipient deposits it in his bank, then the process will start all over again, and even more money will be created.

To see how much money will be created based on an additional dollar of deposits, economists calculate the so-called *money multiplier*. The money multiplier simply equals one over the proportion not lent out (also known as the "leakage" from the deposit and lending process). Thus,

Money multiplier = 1/(proportion of leakage).

If banks always lent out 90 percent of deposited funds and all lent funds were ultimately redeposited, then the leakage would be 10 percent (or 0.10) and the money multiplier would be 10 (i.e., 1/0.10). This implies that a single dollar of currency would turn into ten dollars of total M1 as a result of the deposit and lending process. (In practice, the money multiplier is much smaller than 10, primarily because individuals don't deposit nearly all their cash in checking accounts, meaning that total leakage is considerably higher than 10 percent. Even so, banks still play a very large role in money creation.)

One obvious problem with this mechanism is that if everyone who had deposited funds in a bank asked to withdraw their cash at the same time, the bank would not be able to comply, since it had lent out a large proportion of their funds. Normally, this is not a problem, since total withdrawals tend to be relatively small (and thus manageable) on any given day. But the simple fact is that if a large proportion of depositors demand their cash at the same time (either because they all need it for some reason or out of fear that their bank is in trouble), then the bank will fail. This is known as a bank run or bank panic. Before the introduction of federal deposit insurance in 1933, banking panics were a recurring feature of American economic life.

The Art and Science of Central Banking

Although commercial banks certainly help create money, central banks are particularly important to macroeconomists because they have the power to expand and contract the money supply. Central banks can literally create money at will, and they can also destroy it.

For the most part, today's central bankers regard short-term interest rates, not the money supply itself, as the primary instrument of monetary policy. Typically, they manipulate the money supply as needed to produce the interest rates they desire. If the directors of a national central bank decided, for example, that they wanted to lower the overnight bank rate from 3.0 percent to 2.5 percent, they would announce the change in policy and would increase money growth as much as was necessary to drive the overnight rate down to 2.5 percent. In fact, if the central bank was highly credible, the announcement itself might be enough to drive the rate down to 2.5 percent. Even so, the central bank would still probably accelerate money growth to support the new rate.[10]

Despite the importance of the short-term interest rate, money is actually the factor that central banks control most directly. In fact, they exercise complete (monopolistic) control over the monetary base, including the nation's supply of currency, and they are able to move interest rates only because of that control. If the government ever gave up its monopoly over legal-tender currency, the central bank's ability to set short-term interest rates would disappear as well.

It is a bit like the relationship between the speedometer and the gas pedal on a car. When drivers wish to go faster, they press on the gas pedal and watch the speedometer. Although increased gas flow to the engine is what makes the car go faster, drivers generally set their targets in terms of speed (miles per hour) rather than gallons per hour of gas flow. In monetary policy, although money is ultimately the gas that makes the car go, central bankers generally focus on the short-term interest rate as their main policy instrument, rather than the money supply itself.

In principle, central bankers can use monetary policy in the pursuit of many different objectives. If they believe GDP is growing too slowly or that unemployment is too high, they can reduce interest rates in order to stimulate economic activity. Conversely, they can raise interest rates if they think inflation is too high or is about to become too high as a result of rapid and unsustainable GDP growth (overheating). They can also target a particular exchange rate, raising interest rates when their currency falls in value relative to other currencies, and lowering interest rates when it rises relative to other currencies.

In practice, most central bankers are mindful of all these objectives—vigorous but sustainable GDP growth, low unemployment, low inflation, stable exchange rates, and so forth. Note, however, that there are often trade-offs involved. If a central bank raises interest rates to reduce inflation, for example, it may slow GDP growth and raise unemployment at the same time, a trade-off suggested by the so-called Phillips curve (see "The Phillips

The Phillips Curve

In 1958, economist A. W. Phillips published a major study purporting to demonstrate an inverse relationship between inflation and unemployment. The study was based on nearly a hundred years of British wage and unemployment data. The essential finding was that high rates of inflation were generally associated with low unemployment rates and, conversely, that low inflation rates were generally associated with high rates of unemployment. The *Phillips curve*, shown here, graphically represents the trade-off between inflation and unemployment that Professor Phillips made famous. The precise relationship Phillips identified was subsequently challenged by other leading economists (including Milton Friedman and Edmund Phelps), who emphasized the importance of inflationary expectations and the possibility that a Phillips curve could move over time. Although policy makers might be able to push unemployment temporarily below its "natural rate" by stimulating inflation through aggressive fiscal or

Curve"). An increase in the interest rate may even cause the nation's currency to appreciate, which could further weaken the domestic economy by undercutting exports. Clearly, it is not possible to achieve all of the various objectives simultaneously. In recent years, most central bankers appear to have made low inflation their *dominant* policy objective.

In chapters 3 and 4 we return to the question of what central banks are trying to achieve by raising and lowering interest rates. First, however, we need to identify the tools that they have at their disposal to do this.

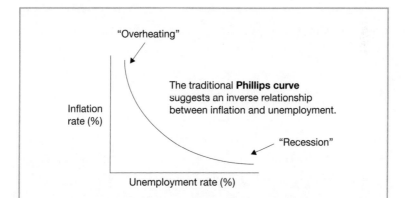

monetary policy, people would soon adapt to higher expected inflation, and unemployment would return to its "natural rate" (but now with a higher background rate of inflation). The "stagflation" of the 1970s certainly proved that inflation and unemployment could rise together, at least under certain circumstances.

Although Phillips's model has since been improved in a number of important ways, a modified version of the original Phillips curve (frequently referred to as an "expectations-augmented" Phillips curve) remains to this day a staple of modern macroeconomic thought.

The Three Basic Tools of Monetary Policy

Traditionally, macroeconomists have highlighted three basic tools of monetary policy. To begin with, a central bank has the power to lend to commercial banks at any interest rate that it chooses. This interest rate, known as the *discount rate* in the United States, represents one of the three basic tools of monetary policy. By lowering its discount rate, a central bank can encourage commercial banks to borrow from it, since they in turn can lend out the borrowed money at a higher interest rate and make a profit on the deal. When commercial banks come to borrow that money, the central bank simply issues new money and gives it to them, thus increasing the money supply. And because there's a money multiplier (based on the iterative deposit and lending process), the initial increase in the so-called *monetary base* (i.e., the money that the central bank issues) will eventually spawn an even larger increase in M1 (i.e., currency plus demand deposits). In this way, the central bank can increase the money supply by lowering its discount rate. Conversely, the central bank can contract the money supply (or slow its growth) by raising its discount rate.

Another tool the central bank can use to manage the money supply is the *reserve requirement* on bank deposits. The reserve requirement—which is set by the central bank—dictates what proportion of every deposit banks are required to hold in reserve (and thus not lend out). Since the reserve requirement represents a leakage from the deposit and lending process (and since the money multiplier is inversely related to the leakage), a higher reserve requirement will diminish the money multiplier and, in turn, reduce the money supply. A lower reserve requirement, by contrast, will raise the money multiplier and thus expand the money supply. In the example given earlier, where we assumed no leakages other than a reserve requirement of 10 percent, the money multiplier was 10 (i.e., 1/0.10). Starting with a monetary base of $100, M1 money supply (including both currency in circulation and demand deposits) would swell to $1,000 as a result of the deposit and lending process. If the central bank reduced the reserve requirement to 5 percent, the money multiplier would rise to 20 (i.e., 1/0.05) and M1 would expand to $2,000. If, instead, the central bank increased the reserve requirement to 20 percent, the money multiplier would fall to 5 (i.e., 1/0.20) and the money supply would contract to just $500. (See figure 2-5.) The point is that a central bank can influence the money supply via the money multiplier by adjusting the reserve requirement.

FIGURE 2-5

The three tools of monetary policy

Discount rate

$\uparrow$ Discount rate $\rightarrow \downarrow$ Borrowing by commercial banks $\rightarrow \downarrow$ Monetary base $\rightarrow \downarrow$ Money supply

$\downarrow$ Discount rate $\rightarrow \uparrow$ Borrowing by commercial banks $\rightarrow \uparrow$ Monetary base $\rightarrow \uparrow$ Money supply

Reserve requirement

$\uparrow$ Reserve requirement $\rightarrow \uparrow$ Leakage $\rightarrow \downarrow$ Money multiplier $\rightarrow \downarrow$ Money supply

$\downarrow$ Reserve requirement $\rightarrow \downarrow$ Leakage $\rightarrow \uparrow$ Money multiplier $\rightarrow \uparrow$ Money supply

Open market operations

Open market purchases $\rightarrow$ Injection of liquidity $\rightarrow \uparrow$ Monetary base $\rightarrow \uparrow$ Money supply

Open market sales $\rightarrow$ Withdrawal of liquidity $\rightarrow \downarrow$ Monetary base $\rightarrow \downarrow$ Money supply

Finally, the third basic tool of monetary policy involves central bank purchases and sales of financial securities on the open market, known as *open market operations*. When the central bank wants to expand the money supply, it buys government bonds or other assets from private financial institutions, injecting cash into the economy. This is called an *open market purchase*, since the central bank is purchasing financial assets. When the central bank wishes to contract the money supply (or slow its growth), it executes an *open market sale*, selling assets to financial institutions and thus withdrawing cash from the economy.

In the United States, open market operations represent the dominant method the Federal Reserve ("the Fed") uses to move the overnight bank rate, known in the United States as the federal funds rate.* The Fed almost never lends to commercial banks through its "discount window." In fact, the discount rate has become largely symbolic, playing almost no meaningful role in U.S. monetary policy. Reserve requirements, meanwhile, are adjusted occasionally, but not often. Open market operations are the main mechanism through which the Fed attempts to influence the money supply. It is worth repeating, however, that the purpose of open market operations—at least in a modern context—is generally to move a particular short-term interest rate (such as the federal funds rate) to a desired level. Although once fashionable, particularly in academic circles, the notion of aiming for a specific monetary target (such as a regular 3.5 percent rate of growth in the money supply) is rarely regarded as an end in itself anymore.

---

* The federal funds rate is the interest rate commercial banks charge one another for overnight lending. It is called the *federal* funds rate because banks typically lend and borrow funds (reserves) that are on deposit at the Federal Reserve. Despite the name, no lending or borrowing by the federal government is involved.

Theory Versus Practice: A Warning

In thinking about the sorts of economic relationships highlighted throughout this book, one very important thing to keep in mind is that they are not meant literally as descriptions of reality, but rather as baselines against which to compare and make sense of reality. A favorite expression among economists is *ceteris paribus*, which means "with all other things constant." If all other factors were held constant as money supply rose, we would expect interest rates to fall. But, as everyone knows, in real life other factors hardly ever remain constant. Imagine, for instance, that just as the Federal Reserve executed an open market purchase to increase the money supply, Americans all across the country suddenly decided that they needed to hold more money—in their wallets, under their mattresses, and in their checking accounts. Perhaps they had just received a warning about a major terrorist threat and thought it would be wise to keep more money on hand, even if this required liquidating some other assets, such as savings bonds or certificates of deposit. Whatever the case, demand for money would rise, and this would place *upward* pressure on interest rates, just as more demand for oil (or any other product) will tend to raise its price. The Federal Reserve might well find that although it had increased the money supply, its action was offset by an even larger increase in money demand, leading interest rates to rise rather than fall.

The point of this little example is simply to remind you that the economic relationships described in these pages (and in the pages of economics textbooks) are not immutable laws of nature. In fact, they break down in practice all the time. If you take a look at data on money supply and interest rates for any country over any significant period of time, you'll find plenty of examples of interest rates rising as the money supply expands and interest rates falling as money growth slows, precisely the opposite of what an economics textbook would predict. But this does not mean that learning about these relationships is useless. Far from it. Only by understanding the baseline relationships can you begin to recognize departures from the rule and, most important, begin to formulate reasoned explanations for what might be driving them.

CHAPTER THREE

Expectations

A final topic of great importance in macroeconomics is expectations. Expectations about the future play a pivotal role in every market economy, influencing in one way or another nearly every economic transaction and decision. As we have seen, expectations can drive an entire economy in one direction or another and can even become self-fulfilling. If depositors expect a bank to fail, it very well might if fearful depositors begin pulling their money out en masse. Similarly, for the economy as a whole, expectations of inflation can produce the real thing; and an economy can fall into recession if enough people expect it to falter. These sorts of expectations are of particular interest to macroeconomists.

The good news is that expectations can push economic reality not only in a negative direction, but in a positive one as well.

Sometimes these favorable expectations emerge on their own. At other times, many macroeconomists believe, the government has to help cultivate them. In fact, managing expectations may well be the most important function of macroeconomic policy, both monetary and fiscal.

Expectations and Inflation

Naturally, neither firms nor individuals want to come out on the losing side of inflation. If workers expect consumer prices to rise in the months and years ahead, they will likely demand higher wages to ensure that their real incomes—that is, their incomes after adjusting for inflation—don't fall. By the same token, if firms expect wages and other input prices to rise, they are likely to try to raise their prices to ensure that their earnings don't fall. Prices and wages will therefore rise in reality as individuals and firms try to protect themselves against *expected* price increases. In this way, expectations of inflation can powerfully drive reality.

One of the main tasks of any central bank is to convince the public that the price level is unlikely to rise by very much in the future—or, in other words, that inflation will be low. This way, expectations can become an ally rather than an enemy. If this is to occur, central banks must be *credible*. That is, for expectations of inflation to be low, the public must believe that the central bank will aggressively and effectively combat inflation (through interest rate hikes, for example) the moment the price level begins to rise too much. Once a central bank achieves such credibility on the inflation front, its job becomes much easier, since high inflation itself becomes much less likely. Conversely, a central bank that suffers from low credibility will find itself in a heap of trouble, with inflationary pressures potentially popping up everywhere all the time.

The reason that credibility of this sort is difficult to obtain is that combating inflation can be very painful. To fight inflation, a central bank typically has to raise interest rates (which likely involves cutting, or at least slowing the growth of, the money supply). As interest rates rise with tighter monetary policy, consumption and investment may slow, since both consumer and business borrowing become more expensive. Output itself may grow at a slower pace, or even contract, and unemployment is likely to rise.

To kill the high inflation of the 1970s, Federal Reserve Chairman Paul Volcker pushed the federal funds rate to unprecedented levels (20 percent at its peak), inducing the worst economic downturn since the 1930s. Real GDP fell by about 2 percent in 1982, and unemployment reached nearly 10 percent that year. Politicians from both political parties expressed outrage. A Republican candidate for the U.S. Senate charged in January 1982 that Volcker's "policy of high interest rates is strangling the American economy and throwing millions of Americans out of work."[1] Although today Volcker is widely credited with having slain double-digit inflation, he was widely criticized (even reviled) at the time he did it.

Had Chairman Volcker been subject to a direct election, he might well have felt compelled to bow to public pressure and ease his assault on inflation. After all, given that he was at least partly—and perhaps mainly—responsible for driving unemployment to its highest rate in nearly a half-century, his odds of winning reelection would have been long indeed. But Volcker, like all Fed chairmen, was a presidential appointee who could not be fired until the end of his fourteen-year term as a Fed governor.

It is precisely for this reason that most monetary economists prefer that central banks be "independent"—independent of the short-term democratic process and, to a significant extent, independent of politicians and politics altogether. Because fighting inflation can inflict so much pain on the public in the short run, elected politicians are often not very credible inflation fighters. Although it is always difficult for those in power to cede control over monetary policy to an *independent* central bank, which could very well undercut political incumbents by raising interest rates at election time, most developed nations have long since taken the plunge—and a growing number of developing nations have done the same. In the United States, the Federal Reserve was not truly independent when it was created in 1913, but it gained additional autonomy as a result of legislation in 1935 and achieved essentially full independence in 1951. The Bank of England, one of the world's oldest central banks, dating back to the seventeenth century, was not made operationally independent until 1997.[2]

Although controlling inflation is normally regarded as the responsibility of central banks, sometimes inflation becomes so virulent that policy makers outside the central bank feel compelled to take matters into their own hands. One extreme approach, which clearly lies outside the domain of central banking, involves the imposition of wage and price controls. If policy makers conclude that high inflation is being driven mainly by inflationary expectations, then wage and price controls may look like an attractive way to change expectations and thus break the inflationary spiral. Why would anyone expect prices to increase over subsequent months and years if the government had declared all price increases to be illegal?

There are at least two potential problems with this approach, however. First, it is unlikely to work unless the government is absolutely credible in its commitment to maintain the controls as long as necessary and to punish violators. Second, and even more important, rigid wage and price controls inevitably create distortions in the economy, thus reducing overall efficiency.

When the supply of a good, such as oil, declines, its price normally rises, signaling producers to produce more and consumers either to conserve on its use, to find substitutes, or simply to be prepared to pay more. If the government prohibits the price from rising, however, buyers will continue to consume oil exactly as they had before until it runs out, leaving others with no access to oil at all. Price controls, in other words, can potentially be effective in shaping expectations, but are often poorly executed and, even when well executed, can wreak all sorts of economic havoc along the way.

One reason why, despite these pitfalls, governments sometimes turn to radical solutions such as price controls is that central banks themselves often find entrenched inflationary expectations extremely difficult to reverse. An obvious solution would simply be to cut back on money growth, starving the inflationary engine of the fuel it needs to run. Unfortunately, since high inflation brings high money demand, an attempt to reduce money supply sharply could potentially send interest rates skyrocketing and thus provoke a severe economic contraction. Imagine barreling down the track in a race car at 100 miles per hour and then suddenly throwing the transmission into reverse. Although the car would indeed slow down, its deceleration would likely be rather violent.[3]

In recent years, many central banks around the world have adopted a strategy of inflation targeting. They pick (and often announce) a specific inflation target—say, 2 percent—and then raise and lower interest rates as necessary to keep inflation at (or near) that target level. One of the many attractions of inflation targeting is that it may prevent an economy from ever falling into an inflationary spiral. If the central bank can be absolutely credible in its commitment to beat back any modicum of inflation above its target, then it may never have to worry about fighting a raging inflation because one should never arise. So long as a policy of inflation targeting remains credible, inflationary expectations—and thus inflation itself—should always remain in check. This, at least, is the theory.

To date, many inflation-targeting programs have proved remarkably effective. One lingering question, however, is how central bankers would react to a major economic shock—such as another oil shock, reminiscent of the 1970s. If inflationary expectations began to rise, would central bankers be willing to induce high unemployment in order to stem the tide? Would they hold the anti-inflation line, or would they falter? Whatever the answer, there is no question that the job of the central bankers would prove a great deal easier if people *believed* absolutely that they would hold the line. Expectations, in other words, remain paramount in determining the effectiveness of monetary policy and, ultimately, the trajectory of prices.

Expectations and Output

Of course, expectations can affect real output as well. The French economist J. B. Say posited in the early nineteenth century that supply creates its own demand—a dictum that has become known as Say's law.[4] Since production generates income equal to the full value of the product that is sold, total income should always be sufficient to buy all the output that is produced. Unfortunately, negative expectations sometimes intrude on this happy circle of production and consumption. If individuals anticipate bad times ahead, they may hold back on their expenditure, including both consumption and investment, thus opening up a gap between *potential GDP* (i.e., feasible supply) and *actual GDP* (effective demand).

The archetypal downward spiral is the result: as nervous consumers decide to save more and spend less, firms lay off workers and reduce new investment so as not to produce goods and services that cannot be sold; rising unemployment depresses income, which further undercuts demand and thus continues and intensifies the downward spiral. Although productive capacity still exists, output falls as productive resources—both people and equipment—are left idle in the face of collapsing demand. Keynes referred to this as the "paradox of poverty in the midst of plenty."[5]

Monetary Policy

One potential strategy for countering such a decline in demand involves expansionary monetary policy. To revive consumption and especially investment, the central bank may decide to lower interest rates (presumably by expanding the money supply). A lower rate of interest may encourage consumption by making saving appear less attractive (since it now pays less) and—what is essentially the same thing—by reducing the cost of consumer borrowing. Similarly, from a business standpoint, a lower interest rate may encourage investment by making new plant and equipment cheaper to finance. In terms of net present value, a lower discount (interest) rate will increase the NPV for any given stream of earnings, thus enticing business managers to reconsider investment proposals that had been seen as nonstarters at a higher rate of interest.

Some economists have worried, however, that under sufficiently extreme circumstances, even aggressive monetary policy might not provide enough stimulus to get a deteriorating economy out of its funk. Keynes speculated that new investment might not look attractive at any realistic interest rate when expectations of future demand were severely depressed.

Keynes also suggested that central bankers might not be able to push interest rates as low as they would like—that is, low enough to stimulate new investment—because of the existence of a "liquidity trap." At a certain point, when interest rates were very low but still above zero, individuals might decide that holding money was more desirable than holding any other asset (since other assets might now be perceived as no longer paying enough interest to compensate for their additional risk). The more money the central bank pushed into the economy, the more money people would want to hold. With money *demand* now rising in tandem with money *supply*, interest rates would stop falling, even as the central bank injected ever larger amounts of money into the economic system. As some economists have described it, pushing more money at this point is about as effective as "pushing on a string." Although the notion of a liquidity trap remains controversial, it nevertheless suggests one means by which monetary policy could be rendered impotent in a depression.

Another potential constraint on expansionary monetary policy is the prospect of deflation. In a bad recession or depression, prices may fall as a result of declining demand. Falling prices can in turn exert perverse effects on the cost of borrowing. Even if the *nominal* rate of interest is somehow brought all the way to zero, the *real* rate of interest will remain positive and potentially even very high if deflation is severe. This is because when prices are falling, a dollar next year will buy *more* goods and services than the same dollar buys this year. For a borrower, this means that repaying a loan—even one with a nominal interest rate of zero— will be costly in terms of actual goods and services. (See table 3-1.)

This is precisely what borrowers experienced in the United States in the early 1930s. By 1932, many nominal interest rates

TABLE 3-1

Real interest rates under conditions of deflation

Real interest rate ≈ Nominal interest rate – Expected inflation

Since deflation is simply negative inflation:

Real interest rate ≈ Nominal interest rate + Expected deflation

Therefore, if one expects deflation (falling prices), the real interest rate will be positive even if the nominal interest rate is zero.

Example: If the nominal interest rate is 0.5% and expected deflation is 10%, then the real interest rate is approximately (0.5% + 10%), or 10.5%.

had fallen to fantastically low levels. The average interest rate on three-month government bonds, for example, had reached 0.88 percent. Still, real rates remained extremely high, since deflation was estimated at about 10 percent that year. The Federal Reserve, meanwhile, kept the discount rate higher than one might have expected (between 2.5 and 3.5 percent in 1932), in large measure to maintain the nation's gold standard. Nominal interest rates for business borrowers also remained relatively high during the early 1930s, presumably in part because of the discount rate but also perhaps to compensate for the additional risk of default stemming from the Depression. In fact, the rates that banks charged on business loans in U.S. cities averaged nearly 5 percent in 1932. This implies that the real interest rate on business loans was about 15 percent, which may help to explain why business borrowing (and private investment) fell sharply at this time.[6]

Ideally, monetary policy would be managed in such a way as to prevent extreme deflation from ever taking hold in the first place. But many macroeconomists believe that once deflation of this magnitude becomes a reality, monetary policy is rendered virtually useless to turn things around.

Fiscal Policy

Another macroeconomic tool government officials have at their disposal is fiscal policy, which rests on government spending, taxation, and budget deficits. Keynes reasoned that if an economy was faltering because expectations of future demand were gloomy, the government could signal better times ahead and thus begin to get things moving again by spending more than it received in taxes and thus running a large budget deficit. As individuals and firms saw the government aggressively creating new demand (by buying goods and services itself), their expectations about the future would turn brighter and they themselves might begin spending again. In this way, the vicious spiral that had taken the economy down could be reversed to bring the economy back up to full employment. The key role for government, according to Keynes and his followers, was to coordinate expectations in a favorable direction through *expansionary fiscal policy*.[7]

Keynes himself described the mechanism in terms of an income "multiplier." Because he believed that a burst of deficit spending by the government would lead both consumption and investment to rise, Keynes concluded that national income (or GDP) would increase by *more* than the original increase in government spending.

To understand this, we need to return to the GDP–Expenditure identity we saw near the beginning of chapter 1. Recall:

$$GDP = C + I + G + EX - IM,$$

where C is consumption, I is investment, G is government spending, EX is exports, and IM is imports. Clearly, if G rises without causing any other variable to fall (Keynes called this an "autonomous" increase in government spending), then GDP has to rise. This is why Keynes focused on *deficit* spending. Had the government financed increased spending through additional taxes, then consumption and investment may have fallen in the face of higher tax rates. But if the government financed the additional spending through a deficit—that is, if it borrowed the additional funds by issuing bonds—then no other expenditure variable would have to decline.

Naturally, if this initial effect were the only effect, then GDP would merely rise by the amount of the autonomous increase in government spending, and Keynes's income multiplier would equal 1 (i.e., the change in GDP would equal 1 times the change in government spending). But Keynesians believe that as GDP rises, individuals and businesses will increase their levels of consumption and investment, thus driving GDP still higher. In fact, this dynamic will repeat itself again and again, as new consumption and investment cause GDP to rise, which in turn encourages still more consumption and investment, and so on.

For convenience, imagine that the effect worked only through consumption. Suppose further that households consumed 80 percent of every new dollar of income and saved the rest. In this case, if the government initiated an additional $100 in deficit spending, the first-round effect would be for GDP (national income) to rise by $100. Faced with an additional $100 of income, households would spend 80 percent of it, or $80, which would thus increase GDP by another $80. Now, with another $80 of income, households would spend 80 percent of it, or $64, which would again increase GDP by the same amount. So far, GDP would have increased by $244 (i.e., $100 + $80 + $64), based on the government's original $100 in deficit spending. But the process wouldn't end there. The virtuous circle would continue to go round and round and round, and GDP would continue to rise, with each increment of growth equal to 80 percent of the one before (i.e., $100 + $80 + $64 + $51.20 + $40.96 + $32.77 + $26.21 + . . .). Eventually, the increments would become too small to matter. In the meantime, however, GDP would have grown by about $500. (See figure 3-1.) Keynes noted that the whole process can be boiled down to the following formula:

$$\text{Change in GDP} = (\text{Change in deficit spending by government}) \times \text{Income multiplier,}$$

where the income multiplier = (1/proportion leakage from the income–expenditure cycle). In this case, since the proportion of leakage (that is, the amount of new income not spent) equals

FIGURE 3-1

Illustration of Keynesian income multiplier

Illustration is based on $100 increase in government deficit spending and leakage of 20%.

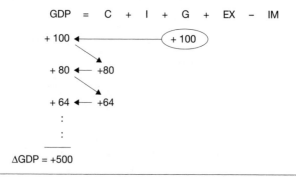

20 percent (or 0.20), the income multiplier equals 1/0.20, or 5. Thus:

$$\text{Change in GDP} = \$100 \times 5 = \$500.$$

This analysis suggests that an increase in deficit spending will increase nominal GDP. In the example given, the increase in GDP is five times as large as the original increase in deficit spending, since leakage is only 20 percent and the income multiplier is therefore equal to 5. What is not clear, however, is whether the increase in *nominal* GDP will come mainly from an increase in the price level (P) or from an increase in the quantity of output (Q). Recall that nominal GDP depends on both of these variables, since nominal GDP = P × Q.

Keynes believed that in times of high unemployment, the increase would come mainly from the quantity of output (that is, mainly from an increase in *real* GDP). In a depression, with many productive resources lying idle, the first thing business managers would do in the face of increased demand would be to put idle resources back to work. They would rehire workers, turn equipment back on, and bring their factories back to life. As a result of all this, production (real GDP) would increase toward the economy's potential.

Eventually, however, if the government kept running large budget deficits even after all or most of the previously idle resources had been put back to work, business managers would respond to increased demand simply by raising prices. This is because it would be difficult for them to ramp up production any further. Nominal GDP would still rise, but now the increase would be coming mainly from an increase in the price level (P), not from an increase in the quantity of output (Q). Economists would say that in this latter scenario, actual GDP (demand) exceeded potential (supply) and that the economy was *overheating*.[8] (See figure 3-2.)

Keynes's proposal to stimulate GDP through deficit spending was thus intended for periods of economic contraction, when real GDP was severely depressed. During more normal times, deficit spending was expected to be inflationary.

Although there were plenty of skeptics in the early days, Keynes's ideas received a big boost from America's experience during World War II. Since the United States finally pulled out of its long depression during the war, and since the war effort involved extraordinary levels of deficit spending, Keynes's prediction that deficit spending would revive the economy appeared to have been confirmed. Keynesianism spread rapidly among academic economists and ultimately became highly influential in policy circles as well. In fact, President Richard Nixon is said to have declared in early 1972, "We are all Keynesians now."

FIGURE 3-2

Keynesian fiscal stimulus, in good times and bad

↑ Government budget deficit ⟶ ↑ Demand ⟶ ↑ Nominal GDP (P × Q), via income multiplier

In periods of **high unemployment**:

↑ Government budget deficit ⟶ ↑ Demand ⟶ ↑ **Q (increase in real GDP) [recovery]**

In periods of **full employment**:

↑ Government budget deficit ⟶ ↑ Demand ⟶ ↑ **P (inflation)   [overheating]**

In **normal times** (modest unemployment):

↑ Government budget deficit ⟶ ↑ Demand ⟶ ↑ **Q & ↑ P (both real GDP and inflation rise)**

Faith in Keynesian deficit spending appears to have waned since its heyday in the 1960s and early 1970s. In fact, there are good reasons to believe that deficit spending may not always deliver as much bang for the buck as many people once learned in their economics classes in college. One reason, as we have seen, is that deficit spending may prove to be inflationary, leading to an increase in prices rather than output. But there are other reasons as well.

In the illustration of the income multiplier given above, the only leakage was household savings. Because this leakage was just 20 percent, the income multiplier was 5. In most times and places, however, the true income multiplier is probably not nearly that large. In part, this is because there are other leakages besides savings. Taxes represent an additional leakage, as do imports, since spending on foreign goods does not contribute to *domestic* GDP.

Some economists, moreover, point to another form of leakage, under the heading "rational expectations." The argument here is that if individuals are perfectly rational, they should anticipate that budget deficits eventually will require higher taxes to pay off the accumulated debt. If individuals wish to prepare for these looming taxes, then they might save *every* dollar of new income derived from deficit spending, thus causing a leakage of 100 percent and driving the multiplier down to 1. Since the underlying idea for this mechanism stems from the nineteenth-century economist David Ricardo, it has come to be called "Ricardian equivalence."

Another problem is that deficit spending may drive up interest rates and undercut private investment and consumption—a phenomenon known as "crowding out." When the government runs a budget deficit, spending more than it collects in taxes, it obtains the difference by borrowing on the open market. It issues government bonds and auctions them off to the highest bidders. In doing this, the government is competing with private borrowers for funds. Naturally, competition for investment funds will drive up the price of these funds, meaning that the interest rate will rise. As this occurs, some potential borrowers in the private sector—including both firms and individuals—may decide not to borrow at the higher rates and simply scuttle the projects they were planning to pursue. Recall that Keynes wanted the increase in government spending to be autonomous—that is, not associated with a reduction in any other form of expenditure (such as consumption or investment). Unfortunately, higher interest rates may cause both consumption and investment to decline, which means that crowding out can reduce—or, in the extreme, even eliminate—the effectiveness of Keynesian deficit spending.

A related issue is that the central bank may itself react to an increase in deficit spending by raising interest rates. Specifically, if central bankers expect the increased budget deficit to be inflationary, they may try to counteract it (and thus preempt the expected inflation) through tighter monetary policy. Once again, such a reaction on the part of the central bank would reduce or negate the stimulative effect of deficit spending.

Nevertheless, despite all of these qualifications and criticisms, most macroeconomists still believe that a small income multiplier does exist. When national economies fall into recession, moreover, most policy makers are still quick to run budget deficits in the hope of getting things back on track. Sometimes these deficits are based on increased spending, sometimes on tax cuts, and sometimes—indeed, most often—on a combination of the two. Either way, a key goal is to stimulate aggregate demand by signaling that brighter days are ahead. If the public interprets the deficit as a sign of weakness rather than strength, the economy may continue to deteriorate. But if—as Keynes hoped—the public interprets the additional burst of expenditure as a good sign, the economy may very well revive on the basis of improved expectations. In a market economy, expectations can literally drive reality, and Keynesian fiscal policy is all about expectations.

Expectations and Other Macro Variables

Not surprisingly, expectations strongly influence other macroeconomic variables as well, including interest rates and exchange rates. If, for instance, a bond trader expects interest rates to rise, she might decide to sell bonds in order to avoid taking a capital loss (since existing bonds generally depreciate in value when the interest rate rises). If a large number of traders follow the same course, long-term interest rates will in fact rise as a result. The sales will drive bond prices down and bond yields (their effective interest rates) up.[9] For this reason, bond markets often anticipate action by the central bank, pushing bond yields (and thus interest rates) up when they expect the central bank to tighten monetary policy and pushing them down when then expect the central bank to loosen.

Similarly, currency traders drive exchange rates up and down on the basis of expectations. If they expect the euro to appreciate, for example, they buy euros (or sell dollars). If they expect the euro to depreciate, they sell euros (or buy dollars). Either way, their expectation actually drives the result. In some cases, they base their expectation on news about macroeconomic data. A dramatic increase in the U.S. trade deficit, for instance, might lead currency traders to sell dollars, if they think the mounting trade deficit makes it more likely that the dollar will depreciate. At other times, traders may be influenced by policy actions. If currency traders expect the Federal Reserve to tighten monetary policy, they are likely to buy dollars, believing that a higher interest rate will make the dollar more attractive and thus cause it to appreciate.

Finally, a word of warning: although expectations are obviously very powerful, one should not conclude from this discussion that they are all that matter. If expectations are fundamentally out of line with reality, they will ultimately be dashed. When, in the 1990s, American investors expected unprecedented performance from Internet companies, they rushed out to buy Internet stocks and dramatically bid up their prices. Eventually, however, when it became clear that the original expectations were overblown, the prices of Internet stocks plummeted (i.e., the bubble burst) and many Internet investors experienced a tough dose of reality.

The same is true of the macro economy as a whole. Positive expectations may help bring a depressed economy back up to its potential. But once that potential is reached and the nation's industries are back up to full capacity, further euphoria will only bring inflation, not a further acceleration of real growth. Expectations matter a great deal, but they are not all that matter. Ultimately, economic expectations cannot survive for long outside the confines of economic reality, as dictated by the technical limits of production over time.

II

Selected Topics–
Background and
Mechanics

CHAPTER FOUR

A Short History of Money and Monetary Policy in the United States

In an attempt to link theory with practice, this chapter offers a brief monetary history of the United States, from the original creation of the U.S. dollar in the late eighteenth century to the execution of modern monetary policy in the early twenty-first. This history illustrates many of the macroeconomic principles and relationships highlighted in the previous chapters (especially chapter 2), and locates them in context, against the backdrop of a maturing national economy. Ideally, you should be able to see monetary economics at work all along the way.

Defining the Unit of Account and the Price of Money

In establishing a new country, one of the first things government officials have to do is define a unit of account—that is, a standard metric for accounting and transaction purposes. The dollar is the unit of account in the United States. In the nation's earliest days, U.S. policy makers defined the value of the dollar in terms of precious metals. The Continental Congress unanimously resolved in 1785 that "the money unit of the United States be one dollar."[1] The following year, the Board of Treasury announced that the "Money Unit or Dollar will contain" 375.64 grains of fine silver.[2] This definition was modified slightly after ratification of the new Constitution a couple years later. The Coinage Act of 1792 set the dollar equal to 371.25 grains of fine silver, or an equivalent value in gold (24.75 grains of fine gold).[3]

In these early years, the U.S. government didn't produce much money itself—mostly just silver and gold coins. Commercial banks produced paper notes that looked official (much like today's government-issued currency) and could be redeemed for coins. Interestingly, these privately issued bank notes functioned as the most common form of money through the early part of the nineteenth century. Later, checking accounts—which economists call demand deposits—became increasingly important. Individuals and firms established accounts at local banks (either by depositing coins and bank notes or by taking out loans) and then could write checks on the accounts to pay for things they purchased from vendors or to withdraw funds from the bank itself, either in the form of coins or bank notes.

By comparison to today, the most striking thing about the government's role in the monetary system during these early years is how limited it was. The federal government did little with respect to monetary policy other than to define the value of the dollar (in terms of gold and silver) and to mint coins. There was no central bank in the United States for most of the nineteenth century. As already noted, paper money was issued mostly by private banks.

Nevertheless, by defining the value of the dollar, the federal government had done something extremely important: it had set a fixed exchange rate. This meant that the price of the dollar would remain stable over time relative to gold and silver—as well as to other currencies, such as the British pound, that were similarly fixed against precious metals. The nation's bimetalic standard (based on gold and silver) evolved into a straight gold standard over the nineteenth century.

The Gold Standard: A Self-Regulating Mechanism?

Although many observers today regard a fixed exchange rate as a heavy-handed form of government intervention, it started out as precisely the opposite. Indeed, a fixed exchange rate (against gold and silver) was the least invasive thing the government could do, short of refusing to create any common unit of account or medium of exchange whatsoever.

Even in the absence of a central bank, the fixed exchange rate was supposed to keep the whole economic system in balance— and to do so automatically. If the domestic economy began to overheat and the country experienced inflation (rising prices), imports would increase (because foreign prices would immediately look more attractive than domestic ones) and exports would fall (for the same reason). As the trade balance deteriorated, precious metals would presumably flow out of the country, since it was often assumed that international traders paid for their purchases with gold and silver. Because the domestic money supply was tied directly to these precious metals, it was expected to fall as domestic reserves of precious metals declined. A declining money supply, in turn, would help to rein in prices, thus counteracting the original inflationary surge. Conversely, if prices fell at home and the country experienced deflation, the balance of trade would improve, gold would flow in, the money supply would increase, and prices would be pushed back up to an appropriate level. This, at least, is how the self-adjusting mechanism was supposed to work.

In practice, however, the system did not always come back into balance very rapidly. Tying the dollar rigidly to gold didn't ensure price stability because the quantity of gold—and thus the price of gold—was itself unstable. Through most of the 1880s and 1890s, as the world's gold supply barely inched forward, the overall price level fell in the United States. Since the price of gold was rising (because of its scarcity), the prices of almost everything else (in terms of gold) were falling. Believing that this ongoing deflation was strangling the economy, presidential candidate William Jennings Bryan urged monetary reform in 1896, declaring, "You shall not crucify mankind upon a cross of gold." Ironically, the world was just then on the verge of a dramatic increase in gold supply. The price level began rising the following year and continued upward for more than a decade.[4]

By 1913, one of the nation's leading economists, Irving Fisher, was so frustrated with the instability of prices that he proposed a radical reform, which he called "standardizing the dollar." As gold fell in price relative to other goods, the gold content of the dollar was to be proportionately increased, so that the dollar would remain stable relative to other goods. Conversely, when gold increased in price relative to other goods, he suggested, the gold content of the dollar should be proportionately reduced, again to ensure the stability of the dollar relative to other goods.

This way, the dollar would never waver in value, and the overall price level (and thus the cost of living) would be stabilized. As Fisher himself explained his proposal, "It aims merely . . . to convert our dollar into a fixed yardstick of purchasing power."[5]

The Creation of the Federal Reserve

Although the government did not adopt Fisher's proposal, major monetary reform was indeed just around the corner. A serious banking panic in 1907 had convinced economists and policy makers alike that a new institution was required, one that would have the power to issue currency at will. In 1914, the Federal Reserve, America's central bank ("the Fed"), was established. Its creators hoped that it would satisfy seasonal demands for money and could serve as a lender of last resort to commercial banks in times of financial distress.

In prior years, interest rates had often swung wildly in response to changing seasonal demands for money, and they frequently had surged to dizzying heights during financial panics. Since the supply of money was so inflexible—tied rigidly to the quantity of gold—changes in money demand (at harvest time, for example) could cause dramatic changes in interest rates.

The establishment of the Fed was supposed to solve this problem by creating a more "elastic" money supply. When money demand surged, the Fed could simply issue more currency to help satisfy it; when demand declined, the Fed could issue less. Initially, the Fed relied mainly on its discount window to inject cash into—or withdraw cash from—the economy, setting the discount rate low when it wanted commercial banks to borrow liberally (so as to increase the money supply) and setting it high when it wanted them to borrow less (and therefore slow or reverse money growth). In this way, it was thought, the Fed could help smooth the business cycle.

Although the Fed had discretion over how much money to create, it did not have unlimited room to maneuver. The law required that the Fed keep a gold reserve equal to at least 40 percent of the currency it issued and that it freely exchange gold for currency at the long-standing rate of $20.67 per ounce. This meant that if currency traders ever believed that too much currency had been issued—such that a dollar was no longer worth its weight in gold, so to speak—they would aggressively trade their dollars for gold at the Fed. As soon as its gold reserve threatened to fall below the 40 percent requirement, the Fed would be forced to raise its discount rate in order to contract the money supply and make the dollar more attractive. The gold standard thus continued to be seen as a crucial source of discipline— a necessary check on monetary excess and a powerful weapon against inflation.

By the early 1930s, however, many analysts had concluded that the gold standard was exerting too much discipline. Even as the economy fell into the Great Depression and unemployment soared, the Fed was reluctant to lower its discount rate too far— and even raised the rate in 1931—so as to avoid sparking a run on its gold reserve. Had William Jennings Bryan still been alive, he likely would have reiterated his charge that America was being crucified "on a cross of gold."

President Franklin Roosevelt sharply curtailed the gold standard in 1933, requiring private citizens to turn in their gold (other than jewelry), ending the practice of exchanging gold for currency at banks, and declaring gold clauses in all contracts to be void. He also depreciated the dollar relative to gold, raising the official gold price from $20.67 to $35 per ounce. One Harvard Business School professor, Arthur Dewing, was so upset about this that he initially refused to turn in his gold and (some say) nearly went to jail in protest.[6] Although a modified international gold standard was restored after World War II, it eventually fell out of favor as well and was dropped for good in the early 1970s. The dollar was thus left to *float* on international currency markets.

Finding the Right Monetary Rule Under a Floating Exchange Rate

With the dollar no longer fixed against gold or any major currency, the key question for officials at the Federal Reserve was how to decide how much money to create. Indeed, monetary economists continually wrestled with this question. Because they kept coming up with new ideas—or, at least, kept rediscovering old ones—"preferred" monetary rules came and went, like fads. Some economists, following Milton Friedman, favored placing M1 money supply on a controlled upward growth path—of, say, 3 to 5 percent every year—to stabilize the price level and ensure a healthy growth rate of real GDP.* Others sought to issue just enough money to stabilize interest rates at low levels—again to

---

* Those who favored this approach and endorsed the assumptions that lay behind it were known as monetarists. A favorite identity of monetarists is:

$$M \times V = P \times Q,$$

where M is the money supply, V is the velocity of money (which may be thought of as the speed at which money circulates in the economy), P is the price level (or deflator), and Q is quantity of output (real GDP). Assuming that V was fairly stable (a controversial assumption), monetarists concluded that the best way to ensure very low inflation and a healthy (and steady) growth rate of real GDP was to put the money supply on a steady upward path, at a rate of increase equal to the rate that economists expected (or hoped) real GDP would grow—say 4 percent per year.

encourage growth without inflation. Still others thought low un-employment should be the target—that more money should be issued in order to lower interest rates and stimulate the economy whenever unemployment was rising.

Although the Fed never explicitly committed to any of these monetary rules, it seemed to experiment with several of them. Most of these rules, however, were ultimately discredited by the high inflation of the 1970s and the financial tumult of the early 1980s. By the 1990s, although the Fed still refused to commit to a specific monetary rule, a rough consensus had emerged among many monetary economists about the benefits of "inflation tar-geting." The basic idea was that central bankers should target a low and stable inflation rate of, say, 2 percent—expanding the money supply whenever inflation threatened to fall below the target and reducing money growth whenever inflation threatened to rise above it.

In fact, in conceiving of how to achieve the inflation target, most economists now focused more on the short-term interest rate than on the money supply itself. Although the so-called discount rate (the rate at which the Fed lent to commercial banks) had long since been abandoned as an important monetary tool, Fed officials had become extremely skilled at controlling one very specific short-term interest rate through open market opera-tions (which involved the buying and selling of government se-curities on the open market). The critical rate in question was the so-called federal funds rate—the rate at which commercial banks lent funds to each other overnight. The Federal Reserve could move the federal funds rate just about anywhere it wanted—usually with extraordinary accuracy—simply by pushing or pulling on the money supply through open market operations.

Naturally, economists who favored inflation targeting believed the Fed should raise the federal funds rate when inflation began

creeping above the target and decrease it when the opposite occurred. Although the Fed would not say so publicly, many analysts
believed it had been following an implicit inflation-targeting strategy since the 1980s. The European Central Bank, meanwhile, had
adopted a more explicit strategy of inflation targeting to guide its
monetary policy.[7] Although some critics charged that monetary
policy was too loose in one market or too tight in the other, inflation had—as of 2006—remained well under control in both the
United States and the European Union for well over a decade.

The Transformation of American Monetary Policy

From the moment Congress declared the dollar to be the unit of
account in the United States back in the eighteenth century, it
became incumbent upon the government to manage money in
some way to make this declaration meaningful—to make the
dollar a reliable metric for transaction and accounting purposes.
Policy makers began by tying the dollar to precious metals at a
specified price. By setting the *price* of the dollar, the government
allowed its *quantity* to be determined by supply and demand in
the marketplace.

One way to think about how money and monetary policy
were transformed in the twentieth century—at least up through
the early 1980s—is to conceive of the government as gradually
shifting its strategy, from setting the *price* of the dollar (and letting quantity vary) to setting its *quantity* (and letting price vary).
Milton Friedman's proposal in the second half of the twentieth
century that the Federal Reserve simply aim for a steady rate of
growth in the quantity of money—roughly equal to the growth
of real GDP—can thus be thought of as the polar opposite of the
original gold standard.

Another—and far more comprehensive—way to think about the transition over the twentieth century is that in setting monetary policy, the government gradually shifted from targeting one price of money (the exchange rate) to targeting another (the overall price level). The goal was always to make the dollar a reliable metric of value that would maximally grease the wheels of commerce without inducing either inflation or deflation. But economists' understanding of what constituted a reliable metric and how best to grease the wheels of commerce changed significantly over time.

Early on, the gold standard was viewed as the best way to ensure a reliable monetary metric, since it guaranteed that the dollar would remain stable relative to gold. The gold standard did not ensure, however, that the dollar would remain stable relative to other goods. As a result, the overall price level (a weighted average of the prices of all goods) fluctuated quite considerably as the price of gold itself rose and fell with seemingly random changes in the global gold supply. Even supporters of the gold standard recognized this problem. Professor E. W. Kemmerer of Princeton declared in 1927:

> There is probably no defect in the world's economic organization today more serious than the fact that we use as our unit of value, not a thing with a fixed value, but a fixed weight of gold with a widely varying value. In a little less than a half century here in the United States, we have seen our yardstick of value, namely, the value of the gold dollar, exhibit the following gyrations: from 1879 to 1896 it rose [and thus the overall price level fell] 27 percent. From 1896 to 1920 it fell [and thus the overall price level rose] 70 percent. From 1920 to September, 1927, it rose [and thus the overall price level fell] 56 percent. If, figuratively speaking, we say that the

yard-stick of value was thirty-six inches long in 1879 . . .
then it was forty-six inches long in 1896, thirteen and a half
inches long in 1920 and is twenty-one inches long today.[8]

As economists became convinced that the right thing to stabilize
was the purchasing power of the dollar relative to goods and services in general (output), rather than to gold in particular, monetary policy clearly had to change.

Today, the Federal Reserve appears broadly to be following a
strategy of inflation targeting, seeking to ensure that the value (or
price) of the dollar in terms of a broad basket of goods declines
(i.e., the price level rises) at a stable rate of about 2 percent per
year.[9] To do this, it manipulates the quantity of money through
open market operations to set one price of money, the short-term
interest rate. It then pushes that rate up and down as needed to
stabilize the trajectory of another price of money, the overall
price level. In this way, inflation should be kept at a modest and
predictable level, and the dollar should remain a reliable yard-
stick—not in terms of how much gold it is worth, but of how
much total *output* it can buy.

Even in the context of money and monetary policy, therefore,
output remains absolutely central—the conceptual linchpin of
modern macroeconomic thought and practice.

CHAPTER FIVE

The Fundamentals
of GDP Accounting

Because output lies at the heart of macroeconomics, considerable attention has been devoted to the question of how best to measure it. In fact, macroeconomists have developed a whole accounting system precisely for this purpose. The goal of national economic accounting—also known as GDP accounting—is to measure the value of all output a nation produces over a particular period of time, typically a year. This chapter provides a quick primer on GDP accounting and the essential challenges and tradeoffs involved in measuring national output.[1]

Three Measurement Approaches

As noted in chapter 1, economists have devised three distinct approaches for determining the value of total output, which focus on value added, income, and expenditure.

Value added. Under the first approach, economists calculate output by summing the value added at each stage of production, where "value added" is defined simply as sales revenue minus the cost of nonlabor inputs (i.e., inputs purchased from other firms). The sum of all value added for every good and service produced within a nation will equal that nation's total output, or GDP.

Income. Since the value added at each stage of production must ultimately be allocated to members of the public in the form of income, another way to calculate total output is to measure total income. Specifically, the returns to an economy's productive factors—labor and capital—can be calculated as the sum of wages and salaries, interest, dividends, rent, and royalties. After a few adjustments (including the addition of depreciation and indirect business taxes), total income will exactly equal total output, or GDP.

Expenditure. Under the third approach, economists measure the value of total output by calculating the nation's spending on final goods and services. A good or service is considered final if it does not represent an input into the current production of another good or service. For example, if an individual buys coffee beans to grind and brew at home, they constitute a final product, the value of which is counted in GDP. But if a café purchases the beans, they are considered intermediate goods and are not included in GDP. Including both the café's purchase of coffee beans and its sales of brewed coffee to the public would constitute double counting, since the price of a cup of coffee includes the cost of the beans.

Whichever method one chooses—value added, income, or expenditure—the aim of GDP accounting is to estimate the value of output, or product. As a consequence, transactions not associated with the production of new goods or services—such as government welfare payments, capital gains and losses, and the sale of used goods—are excluded.[2]

The Nuts and Bolts of the Expenditure Method

Although all three methods for calculating GDP are correct (and ultimately should produce the same result), the expenditure approach—with its focus on final sales rather than value added or income—is by far the most widely used of the three. It gained ascendancy because of its perceived usefulness in macroeconomic forecasting and policy making. As a result, the most common definition of GDP is simply the market value of all final goods and services produced within a nation's borders over a given year.

As we have seen, the expenditure approach breaks spending into four basic categories, the sum of which exactly equals GDP. The four categories are household consumption, investment, government expenditure, and net exports. (See table 5-1.) Thus,

$$GDP = \text{Consumption (C)} + \text{Investment (I)}$$
$$+ \text{Government expenditure (G)} + \text{Net exports (EX} - \text{IM)},$$
$$\text{where:}$$

- *Consumption* includes all household purchases of new goods and services for current use.

- *Investment* includes expenditures that are intended to increase future output of final goods and services. It includes business purchases of fixed structures, equipment, software, and inventory, as well as the cost of new owner-occupied homes.[3] Many countries include government investment—such as spending on new roads and bridges—in this category, but others (including the United States) do not.

- *Government expenditure* includes government spending on goods and services, at all levels of government (federal, state, and local). It may or may not include government spending on fixed capital stock, depending on how government investment is classified (i.e., as government expenditure or as investment). Under neither definition, however, does government expenditure include transfer payments—such as welfare and Social Security benefits—since transfers are not associated with the production of output.

- *Net exports* is simply the difference between exports and imports. Exports are added to domestic expenditure because they constitute domestic output, even though they are purchased by foreigners. Imports, by contrast, must be subtracted from domestic expenditure because they are produced abroad and are thus not part of domestic output.

In most cases, a single item may be categorized in a variety of ways, depending on who purchases it and for what purpose. Consider a coffeemaker, for example. A coffeemaker purchased for home use is classified as household consumption, whereas the same coffeemaker purchased for use in a café is classified as investment. If a café in Italy purchases a coffeemaker made in

TABLE 5-1

Expenditure approach to GDP accounting, United States (2005)

Components of GDP (types of expenditure)		Billions $	% of GDP
Personal consumption	**C**	**$8,742**	**70.2%**
Goods		3,572	28.7
Services		5,170	41.5
Gross private domestic investment	**I**	**$2,057**	**16.5%**
Fixed investment		2,036	16.3
Nonresidential		1,266	10.2
Residential		770	6.2
Change in private inventories		21	0.2
Government consumption and gross investment	**G**	**$2,373**	**19.0%**
Government consumption (G_c)		1,976	15.9
Federal		769	6.2
State and local		1,207	9.7
Gross government investment (G_I)		397	3.2
Federal		110	0.9
State and local		287	2.3
Exports	**EX**	**$1,303**	**10.5%**
Goods		908	7.3
Services		396	3.2
Imports	**IM**	**$2,020**	**16.2%**
Goods		1,699	13.6
Services		321	2.6
Gross domestic product = C + I + G + (EX – IM)	**GDP**	**$12,456**	**100.0%**

Source: Data drawn from U.S. Bureau of Economic Analysis.

Seattle, this counts as a U.S. export and is added to domestic expenditure in calculating U.S. GDP. Conversely, if a Seattle café purchases a coffeemaker made in Italy, this expenditure counts as domestic investment but also as an import, which is deducted from domestic expenditure. Because the investment (a plus) and the import (a minus) cancel each other out, the imported coffeemaker will exert no net effect on U.S. GDP, which is appropriate since no domestic production was involved.

Depreciation

It is important to remember that *gross* domestic product excludes deductions for depreciation. Sometimes called "consumption of fixed capital," depreciation is formally defined as "the value of wear and tear, obsolescence, accidental damage, and aging." (Returning to our coffeemaker example, a café's coffeemaker depreciates in value each year owing to wear and tear from brewing coffee. This wear and tear may be thought of as an input, just like the coffee beans used to make the coffee.) The U.S. Commerce Department's official measure of depreciation also covers reductions of the capital stock stemming from disasters, such as hurricanes and floods.[4]

If capital depreciation is very large across an entire economy, even substantial levels of gross investment may not be sufficient to support rapid growth over the long term. It is for this reason that students of economic development often pay close attention to net domestic product (NDP), which is GDP less depreciation. NDP, or net output, essentially measures the amount of output that can be consumed, leaving the capital stock intact.

In practice, GDP is used much more frequently than NDP. As the Commerce Department explained back in 1947, net product is "theoretically preferable. . . . It suffers, however, from the serious obstacle that there is no satisfactory operational definition of the consumption of fixed capital."[5] Having decided that it was difficult to measure depreciation accurately, the Commerce Department chose to emphasize gross rather than net product, and has done so ever since (as have most other countries).

GDP Versus GNP

Gross domestic product (GDP) measures the market value of all final goods and services produced within a country's borders over a given year. By contrast, gross national product (GNP) measures output produced by a country's residents, regardless of where they produce it.

When Toyota manufactures automobiles at a plant located in the United States, the value of this output is factored into U.S. GDP in precisely the same way as would automobiles produced by General Motors in Detroit. In calculating U.S. GNP, however, Toyota's profits on U.S. production are subtracted from final output. Conversely, Toyota's production in the United States does not factor into Japanese GDP at all, but the profits it earns in the United States are included in Japanese GNP.

In technical terms, GDP excludes net income payments from abroad (sometimes called net international factor payments), while GNP includes them. As a result, "net exports" (EX − IM) is defined differently for GDP than for GNP.[6]

Many analysts consider GDP to be a more useful short-term policy variable, as it appears more closely correlated with employment, productivity, industrial output, and fixed investment than GNP. GNP, meanwhile, may be more informative for analyzing the sources and uses of income. In recent years, many statistical agencies have begun to use the terminology gross national income (GNI) rather than GNP.

In some cases, a nation's GNP may be considerably lower than its GDP (when substantial factor returns are paid to foreign capital or nonresident labor). In 2004, countries with especially low GNP-to-GDP ratios included Nigeria (GNP was 84 percent of

GDP), Ireland (85 percent), and Luxembourg (88 percent). Each of these countries had received sizable foreign investments in their economies and thus paid substantial remittances abroad, reducing GNP. Of course, a nation's GNP could also be higher than its GDP (due to returns from labor and capital abroad). Countries with unusually high GNP-to-GDP ratios in 2004 included Kuwait (GNP was 112 percent of GDP), Switzerland (108 percent), and the Philippines (107 percent). For most nations, GNP and GDP are fairly similar. In the United States, which shifted from reporting GNP to reporting GDP in 1991, the two measures of gross output were nearly identical.[7]

Historical and Cross-Country Comparisons

Because GDP is normally calculated on the basis of current prices expressed in a home currency, adjustments are necessary to facilitate historical and cross-country comparisons.

Controlling for Inflation

To begin with, it is necessary to control for changes in the aggregate price level (inflation) in comparing the market value of output over time. Suppose, for example, that a country's real output (e.g., the number of cars produced, the tons of apples harvested) remained exactly the same from one year to the next but that the average price of every product doubled. In this case, *nominal* GDP (i.e., the market value of final output) would obviously double as well, even though the actual amount of output available for consumption—and thus the nation's standard of living—was left unchanged. To address this problem, economists developed various methods allowing them to control for changes in the price level and thus to produce estimates of real (inflation-adjusted) output. The U.S. Commerce Department first began publishing official estimates of real GNP in 1951.

For a long time, Commerce Department officials relied on a fixed-price method for constructing real GNP (and later real GDP). They selected a base year (say, 1950) and then calculated the value of final goods and services produced in other years using the prices that existed during the base year. In this way, real GDP would not rise as a result of inflation, since prices were held constant. (Simply by dividing nominal GDP by real GDP, economists could also derive an *implicit price deflator*, a measure of the aggregate price level that allowed them to track overall inflation—or deflation—from year to year.[8])

The fixed-price method was not without problems, however. Arthur Burns, a member of the original team at the Commerce Department that helped to develop U.S. GDP accounting (and a future chairman of the Federal Reserve), noted as early as 1930 that a base-year approach failed to account for the introduction of new goods, the disappearance of old goods, and improvements in the quality of existing goods. A related problem was that base-year prices eventually produced a distorted measure of real GDP growth because consumption patterns evolved over time, as consumers bought ever greater quantities of goods whose relative prices were falling.[9] The further away from the base year, the more severe this problem (known as the substitution effect) became. As one observer explained: "Take 1998 as an example: The growth rate of fixed [price] weight real GDP in this year was 4.5 percent if we use 1995 as the base year; using 1990 prices it was 6.5 percent; using 1980 prices it was 18.8 percent; and using 1970 prices, it was a stunning 37.4 percent!"[10]

The Commerce Department sought to address these problems by updating the base year frequently and, especially in the 1980s, by introducing a variety of adjustments for changes in product quality, such as the increasing speed of personal computers.[11] By far the biggest reform came in 1996, when Commerce Department officials adopted a chained method in place of the traditional fixed-price approach for calculating real GDP.[12] Under the chained method, every year became a base year, but only for years that were immediately adjacent to it. Officials could therefore calculate the change in real GDP from 1995 to 1996, from 1996 to 1997, from 1997 to 1998, and so on, and then link all the individual changes into a seamless chain. Because the base year was effectively updated annually, the chained approach did a much better job accounting for changes in the mix of goods and services sold in the marketplace. One unfortunate by-product, however, was that the components of GDP, after being deflated with a chained price index, no longer necessarily summed exactly to real GDP.

Controlling for Differences in Purchasing Power

Adjustments have also been necessary to facilitate comparisons of GDP across countries. Since each country's GDP is first calculated in that country's home currency, national estimates must ultimately be converted to a common currency unit (such as U.S. dollars) before international comparisons can be made. Market exchange rates provide a convenient means of making the conversion, but they can be misleading, since they reflect only those goods and services that are actually traded internationally. Particularly in developing countries, products that are not traded internationally (from haircuts to health care) may comprise a large portion of GDP. If, using market exchange rates, the cost of the same high-quality haircut was $5 in India and $50 in France, then the use of a market exchange rate to convert GDP into a common currency unit would underestimate the value of output in India relative to France.

The standard solution for this problem is to create an index of *purchasing power parity* (PPP), essentially calculating the value of goods and services in each country using the prices of a common country, such as the United States. Continuing with the haircut example, the value of high-quality haircuts in India and France would each be revalued using the price of high-quality haircuts in the U.S. (say, $40). Since the late 1960s, a consortium of international agencies, in conjunction with the University of Pennsylvania, have produced PPP-adjusted estimates of GDP for an increasing number of nations. (See table 5-2.)[13]

TABLE 5-2

GDP per capita, exchange rate versus purchasing power parity (assorted countries, 2005)

	GDP per capita, US$ (market exchange rate)	GDP per capita, PPP (purchasing power parity)	PPP/ER ratio
Argentina	$4,750	$14,550	3.1
Brazil	$4,320	$8,500	2.0
Burundi	$107	$703	6.6
Cambodia	$440	$2,620	6.0
Canada	$35,071	$34,053	1.0
China	$1,731	$6,340	3.7
Egypt	$1,250	$4,180	3.3
Ethiopia	$126	$822	6.5
France	$35,040	$31,210	0.9
Germany	$33,820	$29,760	0.9
India	$727	$3,510	4.8
Indonesia	$1,160	$3,500	3.0
Iraq	$1,060	$2,860	2.7
Ireland	$48,107	$38,552	0.8
Israel	$18,735	$22,676	1.2
Japan	$35,777	$30,620	0.9
Malaysia	$5,000	$10,780	2.2
Mexico	$7,236	$10,040	1.4
Nigeria	$655	$1,250	1.9
Norway	$64,153	$43,310	0.7
Philippines	$1,120	$4,730	4.2
Russia	$5,347	$10,895	2.0
Saudi Arabia	$12,590	$12,670	1.0
Singapore	$26,870	$34,220	1.3
South Africa	$5,630	$12,930	2.3
Turkey	$4,950	$8,100	1.6
United States	$42,024	$42,024	1.0

Source: Economist Intelligence Unit (EIU) Country Data, including EIU estimates.

Investment, Savings, and Foreign Borrowing

GDP accounting is useful because it allows us to calculate the value of current output and to measure changes in output over time. Many economists also believe that it provides important clues about the underlying sources of economic growth and about the sustainability of growth into the future.

Naturally, investment constitutes a critical link between current and future output. GDP accounting not only tells us the value of current investment but also permits us to identify how this investment is funded. As we have seen,

$$\text{Gross product} = C + I + G + (EX - IM).$$

Interestingly, gross product also equals gross income, which—when adjusted to include transfer payments (Tr)—necessarily equals the sum of consumption (C), private savings (S), and taxes (T), since all income must ultimately be used in one of these three ways. As a result, we can say that

$$\text{Gross product} = C + I + G + (EX - IM) = C + S + T - Tr.$$

Some simple manipulation produces the following identity regarding the sources of investment:

$$I = S + (T - G - Tr) + (IM - EX),$$

where $T - G - Tr$ (the government budget surplus) reflects government savings, and $IM - EX$ (net imports) reflects foreign borrowing, since any excess of imports over exports can only be funded through borrowing from abroad.

What this tells us is that investment is funded out of these three basic sources: private savings (personal savings plus the retained earnings of firms), government savings (the government budget surplus), and borrowing from abroad (net imports). If a nation wishes to increase its level of investment, it must either reduce its private consumption (to increase private savings), reduce its government spending (to increase government savings), increase its foreign borrowing, or perhaps do some combination of the three. (See table 5-3.)

TABLE 5-3

Investment, savings, and foreign borrowing (United States, 2005)

	Billions $	% of GDP
Private investment (I) **[= Private savings + Government savings** **+ Net foreign borrowing]**	**$2,057.4**	**16.5%**
Private saving, gross (S_p)	**$1,672.3**	**13.4%**
Personal saving	−34.8	−0.3
Undistributed corporate profits (with inventory valuation and capital consumption adjustment)	354.5	2.8
Private consumption of fixed capital (depreciation)	1,352.6	10.9
Wage accruals less disbursements	0.0	0.0
Government saving, gross (S_G) **[= Government receipts − Government expenditure** **= Budget surplus]**	**−$457.3**	**−3.7%**
Total government receipts (taxes), all levels of government[a] (T)	3,586.3	28.8
Total government expenditures, all levels of government, including income transfers[b] (G + Tr)	4,043.6	32.5
Net foreign borrowing (IM − EX) **[= Net imports = Imports − Exports][c]**	**$771.4**	**6.2%**
Statistical discrepancy	**$71.0**	**0.6%**

Source: Data drawn from U.S. Bureau of Economic Analysis.

[a]Less capital transfer receipts.
[b]Less capital transfer payments and net purchases of nonproduced assets.
[c]Less net income receipts, net transfers in, and net capital account inflows.

Although national economic accounting says nothing about whether any one of these funding methods is better or worse than the others, some students of economic development have suggested that foreign borrowing may be more volatile than domestic savings and may therefore constitute a less reliable source of investment. When a nation's foreign borrowing becomes very large, moreover, critics often warn that the country is living beyond its means, since foreign borrowing (i.e., $IM - EX > 0$) implies that the nation's domestic expenditure $(C + I + G)$ exceeds its domestic output (GDP). This is why analysts sometimes view economic growth as unsustainable when a large and persistent current account deficit—and thus heavy reliance on foreign borrowing—is involved.[14]

In Mexico in the early 1990s, for example, real GDP was growing, but the growth was being fueled (at least in part) by increasingly heavy borrowing from abroad. Many country analysts view a current account deficit of more than 5 percent of GDP as a possible red flag. In Mexico's case, the current account deficit had jumped from 3 percent of GDP in 1990 to 7 percent in 1994. This shift was also visible on the GDP accounts, with net imports $(IM - EX)$ having increased from 1.1 to 4.8 percent of GDP over the same years. Foreign capital, in other words, as well as foreign goods and services, were pouring into the country.

Some foreign investors and many Mexican officials claimed that the huge capital inflow reflected a high degree of investor confidence in Mexico's economic prospects. Yet total investment was falling (as a share of GDP), and consumption was rising. Mexico, it appears, was living beyond its means, importing foreign goods and services (on the basis of foreign borrowing) and using the additional output to increase consumption rather than investment. Although experts disagree about the exact causes, Mexico ultimately suffered a severe currency crisis in 1994–1995, driving down consumption along with the peso and erasing nearly all of the apparent gains of the previous years. A careful review of the nation's GDP accounts prior to the collapse might well have given some indication of the problems ahead.

CHAPTER SIX

Reading a Balance of Payments Statement

Balance of payments accounting is a close cousin to GDP accounting in the field of macroeconomics. In fact, both are essential gear in the macroeconomist's toolbox. Whereas a GDP account reports a nation's output and its component parts, a balance of payments (BOP) statement provides a record of the country's cross-border transactions. As in a GDP account, all of the figures that appear in a BOP statement are flows, indicating the value of exports or imports, income receipts or payments, or new foreign borrowing or lending that have occurred over a particular period of time—typically a year. This chapter presents a primer on BOP accounting and the best strategies for reading and interpreting a BOP statement.

A Typical Balance of Payments Statement

A BOP statement normally includes at least the following line items (or some variations thereof):

Current Account

- Balance on trade in goods and services

  - Balance on merchandise trade (goods)

  - Balance on trade in services

- Net income (net factor receipts)

- Net unilateral transfers

Capital and Financial Account

- Net capital account

- Financial account

  - Net foreign direct investment

  - Net portfolio flows

  - Other capital flows, net

  - Change in official reserves

- Errors and omissions (statistical discrepancy)

Several of these line items require some explanation. Under the current account, merchandise (or goods) are tangible products, ranging from raw materials to manufactured items. Services are intangible products, such as shipping, investment banking, or consulting services. Income receipts and payments include financial returns (such as interest, dividends, and remitted or reinvested earnings) on cross-border investments and compensation (including wages and salaries) for cross-border work. Unilateral transfers (sometimes called "net current transfers") are nonreciprocal transactions such as foreign aid or cross-border charitable assistance (given through the Red Cross, for example).

Regarding the "capital and financial account," the first thing that requires explanation here is the heading itself. Until relatively recently, most countries recorded all cross-border financial transactions (i.e., changes in assets and liabilities) under the heading "capital account." Beginning in 1993, however, officials at the International Monetary Fund (IMF) substituted the term "financial account" for "capital account" and (making matters even more confusing) assigned a new and far narrower definition to the term "capital account." Under this new definition, which is now widely accepted around the world, the capital account includes only unilateral transfers of capital, such as the forgiveness of one country's debts by the government of another country. In most cases, the newly defined capital account is a very small (almost negligible) item on the balance of payments.

The new "financial account" is far more important, since it includes all other financial transactions, such as cross-border trades of stocks and bonds. Although analysts still sometimes use the term "capital account" with its old, expansive meaning in mind (in speaking about "capital account liberalization," for example), most national governments now use the IMF's new definitions of the capital and financial accounts in preparing their balance of payments statements.

As for the items listed under the financial account, direct investment (sometimes referred to as foreign direct investment, or FDI) involves the cross-border purchase of an equity stake in a company—a stake large enough (usually greater than 10 percent) to give the new owner managerial influence in the company. When Daimler-Benz bought Chrysler in 1998, this represented German FDI in the United States. Portfolio investment, by contrast, involves cross-border purchases of stocks, bonds, and other financial instruments (but not in sufficient concentrations to allow managerial influence). Portfolio investment is sometimes referred to as "hot money," since portfolio investors can often liquidate their holdings and exit a country at almost a moment's notice. "Changes in official reserves" reflect increases or decreases in the government's stockpile of monetary gold and foreign currencies (foreign exchange). Finally, "errors and omissions" is a residual category reflecting statistical discrepancies in the compilation of BOP data.

Understanding Credits and Debits

In reading a balance of payments statement (such as the one for the U.S. presented at the end of this chapter), it is important to recognize that every cross-border transaction involves two entries, a credit (+) and a debit (−). Among other things, this means that all of the various positive and negative balances on a balance of payments (BOP) statement must add up to zero.[1]

Naturally, knowing the difference between a credit and a debit is essential. One useful way to think about this is that every *source* of funds (e.g., foreign exchange) is a credit, while every *use* of funds is a debit.

On the current account, exports of goods and services, income receipts (such as interest, dividends, or compensation from foreigners), and unilateral transfers from abroad are all credits because they all may be thought of as *sources* of foreign exchange. Conversely, imports of goods and services, payments of income to foreigners, and unilateral transfers given to foreigners are all debits, since they all may be thought of as *uses* of foreign exchange.

On the financial account, the same basic rules apply. Foreign purchases of domestic financial assets, which constitute a capital inflow (lending from abroad), are recorded as credits, since they provide a *source* of foreign exchange. Domestic purchases of foreign financial assets, which constitute a capital outflow (lending to foreigners), are recorded as debits because they are a *use* of foreign exchange. (See figure 6-1.)

FIGURE 6-1

Debits and credits on a balance of payments statement

Debits (–)	Credits (+)
Examples:	Examples:
• **Imports**	• **Exports**
• **Income payments** (such as interest and dividends paid to foreigners)	• **Income receipts** (such as interest and dividends earned on foreign investments)
• **Unilateral transfers to foreigners** (such as foreign aid or charitable assistance given to foreigners)	• **Unilateral transfers from abroad** (such as foreign aid or charitable assistance received from foreigners)
• **Capital outflows** (such as an increase in domestic deposits in foreign banks or domestic purchases of foreign companies, stocks, or bonds)	• **Capital inflows** (such as an increase in foreign deposits in domestic banks or foreign purchases of domestic companies, stocks, or bonds)
• **Increase in official reserves** (government stocks of gold or foreign exchange)	• **Decrease in official reserves** (government stocks of gold or foreign exchange)
Rules (regarding BOP debits):	Rules (regarding BOP credits):
• **Uses of foreign exchange**	• **Sources of foreign exchange**
• **Increase in an asset** (i.e., an increase in a domestic claim on a foreign entity)	• **Increase in a liability** (i.e., an increase in a domestic obligation to foreigners)
• **Decrease in a liability** (i.e., a decrease in a domestic obligation to foreigners)	• **Decrease in an asset** (i.e., a decrease in a domestic claim on a foreign entity)

A more precise way to distinguish credits from debits on the financial account is to think specifically in terms of changes in assets and liabilities, where assets represent domestic claims on foreigners and liabilities represent foreign claims on domestic residents and institutions. Thus, a deposit held by a domestic resident in a foreign bank is an asset, whereas a foreign deposit in a domestic bank is a liability. *From an accounting standpoint, every increase in a liability or decrease in an asset is recorded as a credit on the financial account, while every increase in an asset or decrease in a liability is recorded as a debit.* When a foreigner obtains a domestic stock, bond, or bank account (three forms of capital inflow), this is indicated with a credit on the financial account, since there has been an increase in a liability to a foreigner. When a domestic resident obtains a foreign stock, bond, or bank account (three forms of capital outflow), this is indicated with a debit on the financial account, since there has been an increase in an asset (a claim against a foreigner).

To see how this works in a specific transaction, imagine that a U.S. company buys a thousand cell phones from a Chinese company and pays for them with a check drawn on a U.S. bank.[2] In this case, we would see a debit (–) on the U.S. current account, reflecting the *import* of cell phones from China; and we would see a credit (+) on the U.S. financial account, reflecting the payment that was made to the Chinese company by check against a U.S. bank. Once the check arrives in China, it represents a claim on the United States and thus an *increase in a domestic (U.S.) liability to foreigners.* Until the Chinese exercise that claim to purchase some sort of American output, their willingness to hold the check (or any other financial instrument into which they could convert it) constitutes a loan from China to the United States—a loan that the Chinese can essentially call at their discretion in the future.

In some cases, one side of a transaction will be misrecorded or not picked up at all by government officials. The errors-and-omission line reflects the net value of all of these discrepancies. It is calculated simply by adding up all of the other lines on the balance of payments and reversing the sign, thus ensuring that all of the lines (including errors and omissions) sum to zero. Often, the underlying mistakes and discrepancies are innocuous. In some instances, however, a large debit or credit on the errors-and-omissions line stems from a large flow of output or capital that is intentionally being hidden from the authorities, such as the import or export of illegal drugs or the surreptitious movement of large volumes of U.S. currency across national borders. When a rich family from a developing country sneaks millions of dollars of cash into the U.S. packed in a suitcase, this secret transfer of capital will show up as a debit on errors and omissions in the developing country's BOP statement and a credit on errors and omissions in the U.S. balance of payments. In fact, when a country suffers a severe financial crisis, one sometimes sees unusually large negative errors-and-omissions numbers on the country's BOP statement in the months leading up to the crisis, suggesting that those "in the know" were secretly removing capital from the country (i.e., engaging in capital flight) before the collapse.

The Power and Pitfalls of BOP Accounting

Clearly, a country's balance of payments can be extremely revealing. One should not be surprised to discover, however, that not every BOP statement is prepared in exactly the same way. As a case in point, the organization of the U.S. BOP statement shown in table 6-1 is a bit different from the generic form presented on the first page of this chapter. Specifically, the current account in

TABLE 6-1

United States balance of payments, 1960–2000 (billions of dollars)

		1960	1970	1980	1990	2000
(1)	*Current account*	2.8	2.3	2.3	−79.0	−411.5
(2)	**Exports**	25.9	56.6	271.8	535.2	1,070.1
(3)	goods	19.7	42.5	224.3	387.4	772.0
(4)	services	6.3	14.2	47.6	147.8	298.1
(5)	**Imports**	−22.4	−54.4	−291.2	−616.1	−1,445.4
(6)	goods	−14.8	−39.9	−249.8	−498.4	1,224.4
(7)	services	−7.7	−14.5	−41.5	−117.7	−221.0
(8)	Income receipts	4.6	11.7	72.6	171.7	346.9
(9)	Income payments	−1.2	−5.5	−42.5	−143.2	−327.3
(10)	Unilateral transfers, net	−4.1	−6.2	−8.3	−26.7	−55.7
(11)	*Capital and financial account*	−1.8	−2.1	−23.2	53.8	455.5
(12)	Capital account, net	0	0	0	−6.6	−0.8
(13)	**Assets, net**	−4.1	−8.5	−85.8	−81.2	−569.8
(14)	U.S. official reserve assets, net	2.1	3.3	−7.0	−2.2	−0.3
(15)	U.S. government (nonreserve) assets, net	−1.1	−1.6	−5.2	2.3	−0.9
(16)	U.S. private assets, net	−5.1	−10.2	−73.7	−81.4	−568.6
	Of which:					
(17)	direct investment	−2.9	−7.6	−19.2	−37.2	−159.2
(18)	foreign securities	−0.7	−1.1	−3.6	−28.8	−121.9
(19)	**Liabilities, net**	2.3	6.4	62.6	141.6	1,026.1
(20)	To foreign official agencies	1.5	6.9	15.5	33.9	37.7
(21)	U.S. government securities	0.7	9.4	11.9	30.2	30.7
(22)	Other liabilities, net	0.8	−0.6	47.1	107.7	988.4
	Of which:					
(23)	direct investment	0.3	1.5	16.9	48.5	321.3
(24)	U.S. Treasury securities	−0.4	0.1	2.6	−2.5	−76.9
(25)	other securities	0.3	2.2	5.5	1.6	455.3
(26)	*Statistical discrepancy*	−1.0	−0.2	20.9	25.2	−44.1

Source: Adapted from the Bureau of Economic Analysis.

Note that on a BOP statement, the terms "assets" and "liabilities" always refer to *changes* in assets and *changes* in liabilities in the year or quarter indicated, not to total assets or total liabilities held as of that year or quarter. On the U.S. BOP statement shown in table 6-1, for example, American holdings of foreign assets *increased* by $569.8 billion in the year 2000 (recall that an increase in an asset is recorded as a debit), and American obligations to foreigners *increased* by $1,026.1 billion (recall that an increase in a liability is recorded as a credit). Although total American holdings of foreign assets and total foreign holdings of American assets are naturally much larger, they are not recorded on the BOP statement.

the U.S. statement is broken first into "exports" and "imports," and the financial account is divided first into "assets" and "liabilities." In addition, the statistical discrepancy line (errors and omissions) appears outside the capital and financial account, rather than within it.

Nevertheless, if you understand the basics of BOP accounting, such variations should not present too great a problem as you seek to make sense of a country's BOP statement. Indeed, figuring out a country's balance of payments is well worth the effort, as it offers a unique window on the country's cross-border transactions and, more broadly, its relationship to the global economy.

CHAPTER SEVEN

Understanding Exchange Rates

For anyone engaged in cross-border transactions, grappling with exchange rates is a necessary fact of life. Although no one can predict with great confidence how a currency will move over a given time period—whether it will appreciate or depreciate, let alone by how much—we can identify key factors that are likely to influence exchange-rate movements, over both the short term and the long term. This chapter offers a brief overview of the most important factors, why they matter, and how they interact.

The Current Account Balance

A country's trade balance—or, more precisely, its current account balance—is one factor that can influence exchange rates. If, for example, a country's consumers developed an enormous appetite for foreign products, the country's current account balance would presumably deteriorate and its currency depreciate. Depreciation would occur as increased domestic demand for foreign products bid up the price of the foreign currencies needed to buy them.

As it turns out, however, buoyant demand for goods and services, whether foreign or domestic, is not the only possible driver of a current account deficit. If, for example, foreigners developed an enormous appetite for a country's *financial* assets, the country's current account balance would deteriorate (the flip side of its improving financial account balance), but its currency would most likely appreciate. Appreciation would occur as a result of increased foreign demand for the country's domestic financial assets (and for the currency in which they are denominated). In this case, a current account deficit would be associated with appreciation, rather than depreciation, of the currency.

In principle, the key question is not whether a country's current account is in surplus or deficit, but rather what factors are driving the surplus or deficit—namely, demand for goods and services or demand for capital. Increased foreign demand for a country's goods and services will likely bolster both the country's current account balance and its currency, whereas increased foreign demand for a country's financial assets will likely cause the country's currency to appreciate even as its current account deteriorates.

Precisely because it is difficult to disentangle these factors in practice, experts frequently disagree on how a particular country's current account surplus or deficit is likely to influence its exchange rate. *In general, though, sustained current account deficits appear to be more typically associated with long-term currency depreciation than with long-term appreciation (and the opposite is generally true of sustained current account surpluses).*

Inflation and Purchasing Power Parity

A closely related factor that has the potential to affect exchange rates is inflation. In general, when one country experiences a consistently higher inflation rate than another, economists expect that the first country's currency will depreciate relative to that of the other country.

One way to understand this is to focus on the trade (or current account) balance—and especially on the domestic demand for foreign products. Rising prices (i.e., inflation) in Country X will make imports from Country Y increasingly attractive to Country X's consumers, assuming Country Y's prices haven't increased as fast. As a result, Country X will see its trade balance with Country Y deteriorate and its currency depreciate (as domestic demand for Country Y's products, and thus for Country Y's currency, grows).

Economists generally view this relationship between inflation and exchange rates through a *purchasing power parity* model of exchange rate determination. The basic idea, drawn from the so-called Law of One Price, is that a unit of currency (say, a dollar) should always have the same purchasing power in one country as in another, excluding transportation costs and taxes. Yet inflation threatens to undermine this parity. If, for example, prices rose faster in the United States than in Britain, Americans would discover that a dollar purchased more in Britain than in the U.S. (since U.S. prices were now higher as a result of U.S. inflation). For purchasing power parity to be restored, the dollar would have to depreciate relative to the pound, until a dollar could once again purchase the same quantity of (identical) goods and services in the United States as it could in Britain. That is, the country with higher inflation will tend to see its currency depreciate.

Interest Rates

Interest rates are yet another important factor that can influence the behavior of exchange rates. In fact, many financial experts and currency traders regard interest rates as the single most powerful driver of exchange rates, particularly over short time horizons.

At a practical level, a country's currency will tend to appreciate when its interest rate rises relative to that of other countries (and to depreciate when its interest rate falls). The essential logic here is that a rising interest rate within a country makes foreigners more eager to invest there, attracted by the prospect of a higher return on their invested funds. The resulting capital inflows drive up the value of the country's currency, as foreigners compete to invest in the country's financial markets.

However, one of the most important exchange-rate models economists have developed seems to predict a very different result. According to the *uncovered interest rate parity* model, if Country A's interest rate rises above Country B's (with no additional investment risk), then we should expect Country A's currency to undergo an immediate appreciation but then to *depreciate* in value after that. The basic reasoning behind this model stems once again from the Law of One Price. For a given level of risk, a dollar (or a euro or a yen) should be expected to earn the same average return regardless of where it is invested. Thus, if a higher interest rate is being paid in one country than another, then investors should expect the country's currency ultimately to depreciate—and to depreciate by just enough to wipe out any excess returns that would have accrued from investing there.

Although this interest rate parity model is conceptually bullet-proof, it doesn't always hold up well in practice. Most studies suggest that, if anything, a country's currency tends to appreciate after a rise in its interest rate and to depreciate after a fall, not the other way around.

Making Sense of Exchange Rates

So what is one to make of all this? Perhaps the most important lesson of all is simply that currency markets are unpredictable—and that this remains true no matter how much training in economics one has. (See "The U.S. Dollar: Defying the Experts.") As a column in the *Financial Times* once observed, "Explaining FX market moves coherently has always been difficult. . . . Ask 10 traders, and you will be likely to get 10 different explanations . . ."[1]

Nevertheless, although exchange rates are often volatile and never perfectly predictable, it is still reasonable to conclude that they are subject to the basic pressures of supply and demand in the marketplace. Since an exchange rate is simply the price of one currency in terms of another, anything that raises the demand for a currency (or reduces the demand for other currencies) will create pressure for appreciation. Anything that reduces demand for the currency (or increases demand for other currencies) will create pressure for depreciation.

A sudden surge in American demand for foreign goods or financial assets, for example, will tend to weaken the dollar (and simultaneously strengthen other currencies). A burst of European inflation would tend to weaken the euro and strengthen the dollar at the same time. An unexpected increase in British interest rates, meanwhile, would likely strengthen the pound, particularly in the short term, though it is possible that the Law of One Price would require a subsequent depreciation of the pound over the long term.

The U.S. Dollar: Defying the Experts

In 2005 and 2006, the U.S. dollar defied the predictions of many of the best in the business, including billionaire investor Warren Buffett and former Treasury secretary Robert Rubin. Both believed that America's massive current account deficits (5.7 percent of GDP in 2004 and 6.5 percent of GDP in 2005) would eventually drive the dollar to depreciate. Although both are likely to prove right over the long term—Rubin said he thought his prediction "was right, probabilistically"—both lost large sums in the short run, when the dollar refused to collapse on cue. Buffett is said to have lost nearly $1 billion for Berkshire Hathaway and Rubin more than $1 million of his own money.[a]

The point is that no one—not even the world's most respected authorities—can know for sure how a currency will move in the future. Making predictions based on fundamentals, including the factors reviewed in this chapter, should increase the odds of getting it right, but certainly cannot guarantee the success of any particular prediction. As Robert Rubin suggested, when it comes to exchange rate forecasts, the very best one can do is to try to be "right, probabilistically."

[a] David Leonhardt, "A Gamble Bound to Win, Eventually," *New York Times*, November 1, 2006.

In fact, the reason why exchange rate movements are so difficult to predict in practice is that currencies are subject to a myriad of pressures at the same time—ups and downs in aggregate demand, currency interventions by governments, interest rate movements, inflation here, deflation there, financial panics, political crises, oil shocks, new technologies, abrupt changes in expectations, and on and on. In general, though, the best predictors are probably:

- *Interest rates* for short-term movements (with interest-rate increases and decreases associated with rapid appreciation and depreciation, respectively)

- *Inflation* for medium-term movements (with relatively high inflation associated with depreciation and relatively low inflation with appreciation); and

- *Current account imbalances* for longer-term movements (with deficits associated with depreciation and surpluses with appreciation, over extended periods of time)

Although there are no perfect predictors, these simple relationships at least represent reasonable rules of thumb for the business manager (or foreign investor or traveler) trying to make sense of exchange rates in an increasingly complex and dynamic global economy.

Putting the Pieces Together

We have clearly covered a lot of ground over the previous chapters. To help keep things in perspective, it is worth returning to the three core concepts of macroeconomics presented in part I: output, money, and expectations. All three—as well as some of the key relationships between them—are represented graphically in figure C-1.

Output

Output, which comprises the goods and services produced in an economy, lies at the heart of macroeconomics. The amount of output a country produces (or, more precisely, its amount of output per capita) determines its level of prosperity. A standard

FIGURE C-1

The macro "M"

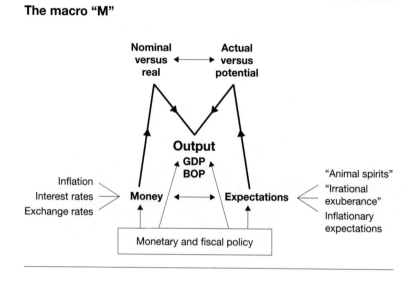

measure of national output is gross domestic product, or GDP. Nominal GDP measures the total value—at current market prices—of all final goods and services produced in a country in a given year. Although a country may temporarily consume more than it produces, it can do so only by importing more goods and services than it exports and by borrowing from foreigners to finance the difference. All of these cross-border transactions are accounted for in a country's balance of payments (BOP).

Money

Money is critical for facilitating the exchange of goods and services within an economy. It can also influence many other important economic variables, including interest rates, exchange rates, and the aggregate price level (inflation). In general, an increase in the money supply is expected to drive down interest rates, cause the exchange rate to depreciate, and increase the aggregate price level.

When the price level rises, nominal values will rise with it, but real ones will not. Nominal values (such as nominal GDP or nominal wages) are measured in terms of *current* market prices, whereas real values (such as real GDP or real wages) are measured in terms of *constant* prices and thus reflect underlying quantities, after controlling for inflation. A 5 percent increase in *real* GDP, for example, means that output—the factor that macroeconomists most care about—has increased by 5 percent, regardless of the inflation rate. Although inflation itself is determined by many factors, money may well be the most important one.

In fact, precisely because money is such a pivotal factor in the economy, governments worldwide assume responsibility for managing the money supply and typically delegate this responsibility to independent central banks. Although they cannot completely control the money supply (since a large part of it is created by private commercial banks in the form of checking accounts), central banks can exert a great deal of influence over the money supply—by determining how much currency to issue, for example. A central bank's primary tools for influencing the money supply are the discount rate, the reserve requirement, and open market operations. In the United States, almost all monetary policy is now conducted through open market operations, which involve the buying and selling of government bonds on the secondary market. Through these open market operations (which expand or contract the money supply), central banks can effectively set the short-term interest rate, which is now widely regarded as the primary instrument of modern monetary policy.

Central bankers typically have many goals in conducting monetary policy. They wish to maintain economic growth at the highest sustainable level; they hope to keep unemployment to an absolute minimum; they aim to keep exchange rates stable; they hope to maintain interest rates at reasonable levels (so as not to discourage investment); and they seek to keep inflation low. Although central bankers would, ideally, like to achieve all of these goals simultaneously, there is now a broad consensus that a primary objective must be to stabilize the price level. One strategy for achieving this goal is inflation targeting, which requires that central bankers raise interest rates (by slowing money growth) when inflation begins to rise above a target level—such as 2 percent—and that they lower interest rates (by accelerating money growth) when inflation threatens to fall below that target.

Expectations

Finally, in all aspects of macroeconomics, expectations constitute a powerful force for both good and ill. As we have seen, expectations can literally drive reality—particularly in the short run. If individuals and firms expect inflation, they may actually create it by preemptively demanding wage and price increases. If currency traders sell dollars en masse on the expectation that the dollar is about to depreciate, their selling—in most cases—will cause it to depreciate immediately. The same is true of interest rates. If bond traders expect the interest rate to rise, they will drive the long-term interest rate upward as they sell bonds in an effort to limit their own capital loss.

Negative expectations can prove particularly brutal when they relate to the economy as a whole. If business managers as a group suddenly become pessimistic about future demand, their gloomy expectation can become self-fulfilling. They might prepare for "bad times" by canceling investment projects and laying off workers, thus causing a reduction in aggregate demand. At this point, the Keynesian income multiplier works in reverse, as consumers and business managers respond to the drop in demand by cutting back further on consumption and investment, potentially setting off a disastrous downward spiral. When this occurs, *actual* GDP falls below *potential* GDP because many productive resources (including both people and equipment) are thrown out of work. Real GDP falls, unemployment rises, and prices tend to decline. (Conversely, if people become overly optimistic about their economic fortunes, they may drive demand far beyond the true productive capacity of the economy. If this occurs, actual GDP will rise above potential, the economy will "overheat," and inflation will increase—all because of irrationally exuberant expectations.)[1]

In a sense, one of the main jobs of macroeconomic policy makers is to manage expectations. During the Great Depression, when real GDP had fallen sharply and unemployment had reached dizzying heights, the British economist John Maynard Keynes recommended aggressive deficit spending (expansionary fiscal policy) to help turn things around. In his view, large deficits would create new demand for goods and services and, as a result, would lead people to revise their expectations upward. As consumers and business managers became more confident, they would increase their own expenditures, setting off a virtuous spiral upward, and the economy would come roaring back to life. (In principle, government policy makers could also cool expectations during periods of overheating by running budget

Basic Concepts, Broad Applications:
From Dairy Farmers to Debtor Nations

A s the reader has no doubt noticed, many of the illustrations provided in this book—such as the one in chapter 2 in which Farmer Bill lends ten cows to Farmer Tom—are contrived. But since they are rooted in truly fundamental economic problems and issues, they should nonetheless prove useful to you as you work to understand real-world economic phenomena.

In our dairy farmer example, Bill lent Tom ten cows at the beginning of the year, and Tom promised to repay the loan in money with 10 percent interest. Since the original price of cows was $1,000 a head, Tom agreed to repay $11,000 at the end of the year (to cover the original ten cows plus one more, as interest). The problem arose when the price of cows increased by 10 percent, meaning that Bill would only be able to purchase ten cows—not eleven—with the ultimate repayment of $11,000. Although this example was useful in illustrating the distinction between real and nominal interest rates, one might regard it as terribly unrealistic. After all, aren't loans always paid and repaid in money? When's the last time you heard of a loan that was made in goods but was to be repaid in dollars?

As it turns out, this illustration is not nearly as unrealistic as it may seem. In fact, the entire U.S. trade deficit rests on precisely this type of loan. Consider the U.S. trade deficit with Japan, for example. Each year, Japan exports more output (such as cars and electronics) to America than it receives in return from America. The difference, which is composed of real goods and services (real output), is actually being lent to the United States. In exchange, the Japanese receive U.S. financial assets, which are promises to repay—in dollars—in the future. Just like the original dairy farmer in our illustration, therefore, the Japanese are lending real output in exchange for a promised repayment in dollars. Ideally, since the financial assets the Japanese receive generate interest and dividends (again, in dollars), the recouped dollars should provide the Japanese with command over more real output in the future, just as the original dairy farmer expected to use the $11,000 repayment of his loan to buy eleven new cows (one more than the original ten he lent). One problem for the Japanese is that if U.S. prices rise in the meantime (that is, if the U.S. suffers inflation), then the Japanese will end up with less command over American goods and services than they expected (just as, after the price of cows had increased, the first dairy farmer was surprised that he could only buy ten, rather than eleven, cows with the proceeds of his loan).[a] Clearly, the dangers of price inflation are not limited to dairy farmers. They are of profound practical significance to all creditors and debtors, including creditor nations and debtor nations all around the world.

Although this is just one example, there are countless others like it. If treated with care, the essential principles of macroeconomics can provide profound insight into economic and business matters, both national and global.

---

[a] Similarly, a depreciation of the U.S. dollar relative to the yen would leave the Japanese creditors with less command over Japanese goods and services than they had expected when they originally made the loans.

surpluses, and thus reducing demand, though in practice the strategic use of budget surpluses has proved relatively rare.

Expectations are central not only to fiscal policy, but to monetary policy as well. By credibly committing to fight inflation relentlessly whenever it appears, central banks can help kill off *inflationary expectations*, thus making it far less likely that their anti-inflation weapons will ever have to be used. Naturally, the same basic idea also applies to controlling deflation. If central bankers make clear that they will respond aggressively to even a small drop in the price level, people are unlikely to expect deflation and, as a result, deflation is less likely to occur.

Uses and Misuses of Macroeconomics

There can be little doubt that macroeconomists have a great deal to teach us about the world. At the same time, it is essential to keep in mind that macroeconomics is a very inexact science. Just as it is dangerous to become overconfident about one's economic prospects or about the prospects of the economy as a whole, it is also dangerous to become overconfident about one's understanding of how the macro economy works. Economic relationships that seem perfectly compelling in theory do not always hold in practice. To give just two examples: interest rates do not always fall when money supply rises, and stagnant economies don't always improve in response to deficit spending.

If this is the case, then why study macroeconomics? The answer, in short, is that macroeconomic theory provides us with a baseline against which to compare and assess reality and, more broadly, with a framework for understanding economic events. When standard macroeconomic relationships break down in practice (such as when interest rates rise despite increased money growth), a good understanding of macroeconomics should help us to ask the right questions and potentially identify what factor or factors might be causing such a departure from the rule.

Unfortunately, some students of macroeconomics are so confident about what they have learned that they refuse to see departures at all, preferring to believe that the economic relationships defined in their textbooks are inviolable rules. This sort of arrogance (or narrow-mindedness) becomes a true hazard to society when it infects macroeconomic policy making. The policy maker who believes he or she knows exactly how the economy will respond to a particular stimulus is a very dangerous policy maker indeed.

The good news is that when interpreted judiciously, the basic principles of macroeconomics—which draw connections between output, money, and expectations—can prove enormously illuminating. Admittedly, we could only scratch the surface of macroeconomic knowledge in this short book. But if you keep your eyes open, you may notice that the basic principles and relationships we have explored here help to shed light on a surprisingly broad range of phenomena, many of which shape the business environment and—more concretely—affect the relative risks and rewards of decisions that all of us (including business managers) make every day.

GLOSSARY

actual output

See **potential output**.

aggregate price level

See **price level**.

balance of payments (BOP) accounts

Summary record of a country's cross-border transactions, typically over a given year. See also **current account, financial account**.

balance on goods and services

Exports of goods and services minus imports of goods and services, where "goods" refers to tangible products (merchandise) and "services" refers to intangible products (such as shipping, investment banking, or consulting services). See also **trade balance**.

bank run

A scenario in which a large proportion of a bank's depositors try to withdraw their funds at the same time, potentially "breaking" the bank (i.e., forcing it into default).

bubble (or speculative mania)

A steep increase in asset prices not justified by economic fundamentals; an unsustainable increase in asset prices that may be followed by a sudden and sharp drop (i.e., a crash).

business cycle

Temporary fluctuations in overall economic activity; temporary departures above and below an economy's long-term growth trend.

capacity utilization

Measures the degree to which a nation's (or a firm's or an industry's) capital stock is actually employed in the production of output. The capacity utilization rate is the ratio of actual output to an estimate of capacity, where capacity is defined as maximum sustainable output given existing plant and equipment and realistic work hours.

capital account

A line item on the balance of payments that reflects unilateral transfers of capital, such as the forgiveness of one country's debts by the government of another country. Prior to the 1990s, the "capital account" on the balance of payments recorded all cross-border capital (financial) flows, but this account is now called the "financial account." See also **financial account**.

central bank

Historically, a bank that provided banking services to other banks and, often, to the government; today, a central bank is typically the institution that exercises authority over a nation's monetary policy. The central bank in the United States is called the Federal Reserve.

consumption

Component of GDP that includes all expenditures by households on new goods and services for current use.

crawling peg

See **pegged exchange rate**.

crowding out

The reduction in private investment that may ensue when the government runs a budget deficit. Note that a budget deficit (i.e., new government borrowing) implies increased government demand for investment funds, which may "crowd out" private investment by bidding up the interest rate faced by private investors.

currency

The most liquid form of money, including bills and coins, typically issued by the government. Currency is said to be "in circulation" when it is held outside of a bank vault. The term "currency" may also be used to refer to a national unit of account—such as the U.S. dollar or the Mexican peso.

current account

A major item on the balance of payments that records a country's international transactions for current use, including net exports of goods and services, net income, and net transfers; the current account also reflects the amount of net lending to foreigners (or, in the case of a current account deficit, net borrowing from foreigners).

cyclical fluctuations

Temporary departures from the long-term (secular) trend of an economic variable. See also **secular trend**.

deficit spending

Government spending financed on the basis of borrowed funds, rather than tax revenues.

demand deposit

A bank account, such as a checking account, in which the deposited funds can be withdrawn or transferred by the account holder on demand.

depreciation

Decrease in value of fixed capital owing to wear and tear, damage or destruction, or obsolescence. The term "depreciation" may also be used in relation to a national currency or other financial asset to indicate decline in value due to market conditions.

depression

An extended period of economic stagnation or contraction, typically characterized by very low or negative real GDP growth, high unemployment, and low capacity utilization. See also **recession**.

discount rate

The rate of interest that a central bank charges on loans to commercial banks. Traditionally, central banks made these loans by buying assets from commercial banks at a small discount—hence the term "discount rate."

errors and omissions

A residual category on the balance of payments reflecting statistical discrepancies in the compilation of BOP data.

exchange rate

The price of one national currency in terms of another (e.g., the number of Japanese yen needed to purchase one U.S. dollar).

exchange rate peg

See **pegged exchange rate**, **fixed exchange rate**.

expenditure method

A method for calculating GDP, based on expenditures for final goods and services. According to this approach a country's GDP equals the sum of its consumption expenditures, investment expenditures, government expenditures, and net exports (exports minus imports).

exports

Foreign purchases of domestically produced goods and services.

federal funds rate

A key short-term interest rate in the U.S. that the Federal Reserve targets in setting monetary policy; specifically, the rate that commercial banks in the U.S. charge each other on overnight loans.

final goods and services

Output that is expected to be used (in the current year) and not resold.

financial account

A major item on the balance of payments that records a country's international financial transactions, including net flows of foreign direct investment and portfolio investment.

fiscal policy

Use of government taxation or spending to influence macroeconomic performance (GDP growth, unemployment, inflation, etc.).

fixed exchange rate

An exchange rate that is officially set by a national government or central bank, typically by promising to buy or sell the national currency for foreign exchange reserves, on demand, at the fixed rate. See also **floating exchange rate**, **gold standard**.

floating exchange rate (or flexible exchange rate)

An exchange rate that is permitted to move freely (appreciate or depreciate), based on supply and demand conditions within the global marketplace. In a pure floating regime, the government never uses its foreign currency reserves to stabilize (or otherwise influence) the exchange rate. See also **fixed exchange rate**.

foreign borrowing

Capital inflows from abroad. These inflows (or borrowing) may take many forms, including foreign deposits in domestic banks, foreign purchases of domestic securities (including stocks and bonds), foreign direct investment (including foreign purchases of domestic companies), and so forth. A country engages in net borrowing from abroad whenever its current account is in deficit, which broadly indicates that the country's expenditures exceed its production of output.

foreign direct investment (FDI)

Involves the cross-border purchase of an equity stake in a company that is large enough (usually greater than 10 percent) to give the foreign owner managerial influence in the company. When Daimler-Benz bought Chrysler in 1998, this represented German FDI in the United States. See also **portfolio investment**.

funded pension system

A retirement program in which workers save for their own retirement (or in which other parties, such as their employers, save on their behalf) by purchasing financial assets, from which the workers will derive income when they retire.

gold standard

A type of fixed exchange rate in which the price of a currency is officially set (or fixed) in terms of gold. For example, from 1946 to 1971, the U.S. government set the price of the U.S. dollar at $35 per ounce of gold (although in this case only foreign central banks—not individuals or firms—were permitted to exchange dollars for gold at this rate). See also **fixed exchange rate**.

government expenditure

Component of GDP that includes all government spending on goods and services, at all levels of government (federal, state, and local), but does not include transfer payments (such as welfare or social security benefits). The definition may or may not include government spending on fixed capital stock, depending on how the country in question classifies government investment (i.e., as government expenditure or as investment). See also **investment**.

Great Depression

The long period of economic decline and stagnation that characterized the 1930s in many countries around the world.

gross domestic product (GDP)

The most widely accepted measure of a country's total output; often defined as the market value of all final goods and services produced within a country over a given year. See also **gross national product**, **depreciation**.

gross national product (GNP)

The market value of all final goods and services produced by a country's residents over a given year, regardless of where the output is produced (i.e., at home or abroad). In technical terms, gross national product (GNP) includes net income receipts from abroad (sometimes called net international factor receipts), while gross domestic product (GDP) excludes them. See also **gross domestic product**.

hot money

See **portfolio investment**.

imports

Domestic purchases of foreign-produced goods and services.

income

Payment to labor and capital for their respective contributions to the production of output; distributed in the form of wages and salaries, profit, interest, rent, and royalties.

income multiplier

The ratio of expected change in GDP to the autonomous change in expenditure used to generate it. E.g., if a $100 increase in government deficit spending ultimately leads to a $200 increase in GDP, then the income multiplier would be $200/$100, or 2.

inflation

An increase in the average level of prices across an economy. The term is sometimes used as a shorthand for "consumer price inflation," which refers to an increase in the average level of *consumer* prices (as reflected, for example, by an increase in the cost of a representative basket of consumer goods).

inflation targeting

A monetary strategy in which a central bank aims to keep the rate of inflation at or near a target (e.g., 2 percent), typically by raising or lowering the short-term interest rate, as needed.

inflationary expectations

Assumptions (or predictions) about future changes in the price level (i.e., future inflation).

investment

Component of GDP that includes all expenditures intended to increase future output of final goods and services. Investment expenditures typically include business purchases of fixed structures, equipment, software, and inventory, as well as the cost of new owner-occupied homes. Many countries include government investment—such as spending on new roads and bridges—in this category, but others (including the United States) do not.

labor productivity

See **productivity**.

Laffer curve

A graphic representation of the relationship between tax rates and tax revenues (originally suggested by economist Arthur Laffer), in which revenues are shown to be zero at tax rates of both 0 percent and 100 percent; often used to suggest that tax revenues may rise when tax rates are reduced from sufficiently high levels.

lender of last resort

An institution—often a public institution, such as a central bank—that is able and willing to lend to financial institutions (and particularly to banks) during liquidity crises, when other potential lenders in the private sector are either unwilling or unable to lend.

liquidity trap

A scenario suggested by the British economist John Maynard Keynes in which monetary policy could prove impotent, particularly within the context of a financial crisis. If, in the face of very low interest rates, central bankers find it impossible to lower interest rates further through open market purchases (i.e., by purchasing government bonds with newly issued currency), then monetary policy will no longer be an effective tool for stimulating additional consumption and investment. As some economists have described it, pushing more money at this point is about as effective as "pushing on a string."

monetary base

Equal to the total liabilities of the central bank; includes all currency outstanding plus commercial bank deposits at the central bank (known as reserves).

monetary policy

The efforts of a central bank to influence economic performance (for example, to maintain a target rate of inflation) through manipulation of the money supply and short-term interest rates.

money

A medium of exchange that is widely accepted as payment for goods and services and in financial transactions; a highly liquid form of wealth that is itself a means of payment or is easily converted into a means of payment.

money identity

$M \times V = P \times Q$, where M is the money supply, V is the velocity of money, P is the price level, and Q is the quantity of output produced (i.e., real GDP). See also **money supply**, **velocity of money**, **price level**, **real**.

money illusion

A phenomenon whereby individuals confuse nominal and real values—e. g., mistakenly view changes in their *nominal* wage, uncorrected for changes in the price level (inflation or deflation), as an accurate measure of changes in their *real* purchasing power.

money multiplier

The ratio of the total money supply to the monetary base. If the money multiplier is 2 and the central bank increases the monetary base (i.e., its liabilities) by $100, then we would expect total money supply to rise by $200. See also **money supply**, **monetary base**.

money supply (or money stock)

The quantity of money at a particular moment in time. Economists define a range of monetary aggregates—M1, M2, M3, and so forth—that correspond to progressively broader notions of money. For example, whereas M1 includes currency in circulation and demand deposits, M2 includes currency in circulation and demand deposits *as well as* time deposits (or savings accounts).

national economic accounts

Another name for the GDP accounts, which normally include measures of GDP as well as its major components (consumption, investment, government expenditure, exports, and imports).

natural rate of unemployment

Also known as the nonaccelerating inflation rate of unemployment (NAIRU), it is the rate of unemployment below which inflation is likely to accelerate.

net domestic product (NDP)

Gross domestic product (GDP), less depreciation of the capital stock. See also **gross domestic product**.

net exports

Exports minus imports. See also **exports**, **imports**.

net factor receipts

See **net income**.

net income (or net factor receipts)

Income receipts minus income payments in the current account of the balance of payments. Income receipts include compensation paid by foreigners to domestic residents (e.g., for work done abroad), interest and dividends from foreigners on domestic holdings of foreign assets, and reinvested earnings on foreign direct investment (FDI) abroad; income payments include compensation paid to foreigners by domestic residents (or firms), interest and dividends paid to foreigners on foreign holdings of domestic assets, and reinvested earnings on FDI in the domestic economy.

net present value (NPV)

The present discounted value of the revenues from a project minus the present discounted value of its costs; used to assess the project's expected profitability.

net unilateral transfers (or net transfers)

An element of the current account on the balance of payments that reflects nonreciprocal transactions such as foreign aid or cross-border charitable assistance (given through the Red Cross, for example).

nominal

A measure expressed in (or relative to) current market prices and thus uncorrected for inflation—e.g., nominal GDP, nominal wage, nominal interest rate, nominal exchange rate. See also **real**.

official reserves

An element of the financial account on the balance of payments that reflects increases or decreases in the government's stockpile of foreign currencies (foreign exchange) and monetary gold.

open market operations

The purchase or sale of securities on the open market by the central bank, for the purpose of raising or lowering the monetary base (and thus lowering or raising the short-term interest rate).

output

The goods and services produced in an economy.

overheating

Rapid and unsustainable GDP growth, in which actual GDP exceeds potential GDP; typically associated with rising inflation.

pay-as-you-go pension system

A retirement program, often run by the government, in which benefits are paid to current retirees solely on the basis of current contributions from—or taxes levied on—current workers (i.e., future retirees).

pegged exchange rate

Generally the same as a fixed exchange rate (see **fixed exchange rate**). However, under a "crawling peg," the official exchange rate (i.e., the peg) is allowed to change gradually over time (e.g., by a small percentage per month) and, in some cases, is allowed to float within a narrow band, the boundaries of which are themselves allowed to change gradually over time.

Phillips curve

A graphical representation of the apparent trade-off between the rate of unemployment and the rate of inflation; based on an empirical finding first highlighted by economist A. W. Phillips.

portfolio investment (or portfolio flows)

Involves cross-border purchases of stocks, bonds, and other financial instruments, but not in sufficient concentrations to allow managerial influence. Portfolio investment is sometimes referred to as "hot money," since portfolio investors can often liquidate their holdings and exit a country at almost a moment's notice.

potential output

The output (GDP) an economy could produce, given the existing state of technology, if all of its resources (labor and capital) were employed at a sustainable level of intensity. When actual output is significantly below potential output, the economy is said to be in recession; when actual output is significantly greater than potential output, the economy is said to be overheating.

price deflator (or price index)

A measure of the price level. The GDP price deflator (P) equals nominal GDP divided by real GDP. See also **price level**.

price level

Essentially the average of all prices (or a subset thereof) at a given moment in time. The percentage change in the price level from one year to the next is the annual inflation rate.

price rigidity

Prices are said to be "rigid" (or "sticky") when they do not immediately adjust to bring supply and demand into balance in the face of changing market conditions.

productivity

Output per unit of input. The term is often used as a shorthand for "labor productivity," which is defined as output per worker or output per worker hour. See also **total factor productivity**.

purchasing power parity (PPP)

Drawn from the Law of One Price, the PPP model of exchange-rate determination holds that a unit of currency should always have the same purchasing power in one country as in another, excluding transportation costs and taxes. If PPP exists between two countries, and Country A then experiences higher inflation than Country B, the PPP model predicts that Country A's currency will have to depreciate relative to Country B's until parity is restored. One shortcoming of this model is that markets do not ensure that the Law of One Price holds for goods and services that are not traded in the international marketplace. To address this, economists have created PPP indexes that estimate the purchasing power of a common unit of currency (typically a dollar) with respect to all goods and services—both those that are traded internationally (such as cars) and those that are not (such as haircuts). If Country X has a PPP index of 1.5 relative to the U.S. dollar, then $1.00 worth of Currency X (at market exchange rates) would be able to purchase goods and services in Country X worth $1.50 in the United States. As a result, adjusting GDP per capita according to a PPP index, rather than on the basis of market exchange rates alone, may provide a more meaningful comparison of living standards across countries.

rational expectations

Expectations (or forecasts) that are based on all available information and that avoid systematic errors.

real

A measure expressed in (or relative to) constant prices, and thus corrected for inflation (e.g., real GDP, real wage, real interest rate, real exchange rate). See also **nominal**.

real exchange rate

A measure that adjusts the nominal exchange rate between two countries to control for differences in inflation between those two countries. If the nominal exchange rate of Currency A in terms of Currency B has been stable, but Country A has experienced sharply higher inflation than Country B, then Country A's *real* exchange rate will have appreciated.

recession

A period of general economic contraction, typically characterized by negative real GDP growth, a higher-than-normal unemployment rate, and a lower-than-normal capacity utilization rate. Although there is no universally accepted definition of a recession, one rule of thumb is that a recession involves at least two consecutive quarters of negative real GDP growth.

reserve requirement

The proportion of total deposits that a bank must, by law, hold on reserve (and thus not lend out). These reserves are generally held as deposits at the central bank.

Ricardian equivalence

The notion that individuals will react to a government budget deficit by increasing current savings (rather than consumption), based on their rational expectation that increased government borrowing today will require higher taxes in the future. If true, this response on the part of individuals would limit or potentially negate the effects of expansionary fiscal policy.

secular trend

The long-term direction or trajectory of an economic variable. See also **cyclical fluctuations**.

sticky wages

Wages are said to be "sticky" when they do not immediately adjust to bring supply and demand into balance in the face of changing market conditions. They are said to be "sticky on the downside" when they rise more easily than they fall, even in the face of precisely opposite market pressures. See also **price rigidity**.

total factor productivity

A measure of the efficiency with which labor and capital are used in producing output in an economy. An increase in output that is not attributable to an increase in either labor or capital is attributed, by definition, to an increase in total factor productivity.

trade balance

Exports minus imports. This may refer either to the balance on goods (merchandise) or to the balance on goods and services.

transfer payments

Payments—typically by governments in the form of welfare or social security benefits—that are not associated with the production of output. Transfer payments are not counted as part of government expenditure (G) in calculating GDP.

unemployment rate

The percentage of people in the labor force who are not working but are actively looking for work.

unit labor costs (ULC)

Employee compensation per unit of output produced. Unit labor costs rise when compensation costs increase faster than labor productivity, and fall when compensation costs increase more slowly than labor productivity.

value added

The value of output as measured by its sales price, less the cost of the nonlabor inputs used to produce it.

velocity of money

The ratio of nominal GDP (P × Q) to the money supply (M); sometimes characterized loosely as the speed at which money circulates within an economy.

wage and price controls

Legal restrictions on allowable movements (changes) of wages, prices, or both.

NOTES

Chapter One

1. Products that remain unsold are also counted as part of GDP. Specifically, they are classified as additions to business inventory and thus as an implicit form of business expenditure (investment).

2. Ideally, the electric saw would be added to national output when it was first purchased (as investment) and then gradually subtracted from output as it depreciates (that is, as it is itself consumed in the production process). This approach would yield a net measure of national output (i.e., net of depreciation), commonly called net domestic product, or NDP. Because depreciation can be difficult to measure, however, it is often ignored in calculating national output. As a result, economists and policy makers typically rely more heavily on *gross* domestic product (GDP) than on *net* domestic product (NDP).

3. It is important to remember that income is not the same as wealth. Your income is the amount you earn each year, through your employment and the distributed returns on your investments. Wealth reflects the investments themselves, derived from your accumulated savings over all previous years.

4. Another reason why countries sometimes wish to run trade surpluses (and aggressively pursue foreign markets) is to increase demand for domestically produced goods and services—or, to put it another way, to ensure an outlet for their production. We will return to the concept of aggregate demand management later in this chapter and in chapter 3.

5. The classic example of how efficiency can be increased through reorganization and specialization of tasks comes from the eighteenth-century economist Adam Smith. Smith maintained that the proper division of labor could sharply increase efficiency. Illustrating this point by describing how pins are made, he observed that "a workman not educated to this business [of pin making] . . . could scarce, perhaps, with his utmost industry, make one pin in a day, and certainly could not make

twenty." He proceeded to explain, however, that when tasks were appropriately divided and allocated among ten workers, they were able to produce "upwards of forty-eight thousand pins in a day." The trick was for each worker to specialize: "One man draws out the wire, another straights it, a third cuts it, a fourth points it, a fifth grinds it at the top for receiving the head" and so on. See Adam Smith, *An Inquiry into the Nature and Causes of the Wealth of Nations* (1776), bk. I, ch. 1, para. 3.

6. Herbert Hoover, address to the American Bankers' Association, Oct. 2, 1930.

7. Franklin Roosevelt, inaugural address, March 4, 1933.

8. John Maynard Keynes, *The Means to Prosperity* (New York: Harcourt Brace, 1933).

9. Some types of wealth—such as inventories of corn or other agricultural products—can actually be consumed directly, but most cannot.

10. Economist Intelligence Unit (estimates of GDP per capita in US$ at market exchange rates). Based on a purchasing power parity (PPP) measure, GDP per capita was $703 in Burundi and $822 in Ethiopia in 2005. On purchasing power parity, see chapter 5.

Chapter Two

1. David Hume, "Of Money," in *Political Discourses* (1752).

2. It is not hard to see that the deflator had to equal 1.00 in 2005, since we selected 2005 as the base year in this example (i.e., the year from which a constant set of prices was derived). A standard convention for presenting price deflators (in macroeconomic charts and tables) is to multiply them by 100. A deflator of 1.00 would thus be presented as 100, and a deflator of 2.00 as 200.

3. When, in rare circumstances, short-term rates exceed long-term rates, the yield curve is said to be inverted. Some economists interpret an inverted yield curve as a sign of an impending recession.

4. An annual interest rate of 1,000 percent may seem fanciful. However, loan sharks and other predatory lenders often charge exorbitant rates—in this range and even higher—on short-term loans to cash-starved borrowers. Note that a *daily* interest rate of just 0.66 percent is equivalent to an *annual* rate of approximately 1,000 percent. In fact, predatory lending of this sort is more common than generally thought. The U.S. Department of Defense, for example, reported in 2006 that predatory lending targeting members of the armed forces was "preva-

lent." Of particular concern were so-called payday loans, in which military personnel borrowed small sums for approximately two weeks until "the next payday" at interest rates ranging from 390 percent to 780 percent on an annual basis. See U.S. Department of Defense, *Report on Predatory Lending Practices Directed at Members of the Armed Forces and Their Dependents* (Washington, DC, August 9, 2006), esp. 10.

5. Although inflations of this magnitude are rare, they are not unheard of. Since 1970, more than a dozen countries have experienced annual inflation of greater than 1,000 percent, including (among others) Angola, Argentina, Bolivia, Brazil, Democratic Republic of the Congo, Croatia, Kazakhstan, Peru, and Ukraine. During Israel's triple-digit inflation of the early 1980s, an oft-repeated joke asked whether it was better to travel from Tel Aviv to Jerusalem by bus or cab. The answer: in a time of extreme inflation, it is better to travel by cab, since the traveler pays for the bus at the beginning of the trip but for the cab at the end (by which time, presumably, one's money had already depreciated in value).

6. Under its exchange-rate peg, the Mexican central bank committed to maintain the peso–dollar exchange rate within a relatively narrow band (by agreeing to buy or sell pesos for dollars, as needed, at prices within the band). This gave many foreign investors confidence that, so long as the peg held, they would not face a sharp depreciation of the peso.

7. Irving Fisher, *The Money Illusion* (New York: Adelphi Co., 1928).

8. Although the Federal Reserve decides how much currency will be issued, it does not actually print the currency itself. That task is left to the U.S. Treasury—more specifically, to the Bureau of Engraving and Printing (bills) and the U.S. Mint (coins).

9. At the end of 2005, M1 money supply totaled approximately $1.4 trillion. A broader definition of the money supply, known as M2, includes currency in circulation and demand deposits *as well as* time deposits (or savings accounts). At the end of 2005, savings accounts (including small-denomination CDs and money market funds) totaled $5.3 trillion, which brought the total M2 money supply to $6.7 trillion. A still broader definition of money, known as M3, includes everything in M2 as well as such things as large denomination time deposits (i.e., CDs over $100,000), overnight and term repurchase agreements (repos), and overnight and term Eurodollar accounts. Including these items added another $3.5 trillion to the money supply in 2005, bringing M3 to $10.2 trillion. See *Economic Report of the President 2006* (Washington, DC: GPO, 2006), tables b-69 and b-70.

10. Recall that since the interest rate may be thought of as the price of money (or, more precisely, the price of purchasing money for a period of time), an increase in the supply of money will tend to lower that price (i.e., lower the interest rate), just as an increase in the supply of any good tends to lower the price of that good.

Chapter Three

1. Joseph F. Sullivan, "Bell Joins G.O.P. Primary for the Senate in Jersey," *New York Times*, 28 Jan 1982, sec. B.

2. Although the Bank of England became "operationally independent" in 1997 after being granted responsibility for setting short-term interest rates, it still lacked complete independence. The British government retained the authority to set the overall inflation target, which the Bank was expected to meet.

3. Although Paul Volcker essentially did this in the United States in the early 1980s, he was confronting an inflation rate of less than 20 percent. In many countries, inflation rates have reached far higher levels— sometimes as high as 1,000 percent per year or more. In Brazil, for example, inflation in 1990 exceeded 2,500 percent.

4. Say himself expressed the idea this way: "[A] product is no sooner created, than it, from that instant, affords a market for other products to the full extent of its own value" [Jean-Baptiste Say, *A Treatise on Political Economy*, trans. C. R. Prinsep, ed. Clement C. Biddle (Philadelphia: Lippincott, Grambo & Co., 1855 {1803}): bk. I, chap. XV, para. 8]. Although the idea was developed by other classical economists (including James Mill, David Ricardo, and John Stuart Mill), the actual phrase "supply creates its own demand," now known as Say's law, was coined later— perhaps as late as 1936 by John Maynard Keynes, who was attacking the idea. See Keynes, *The General Theory of Employment, Interest, and Money* (New York: Harcourt Brace Jovanovich, 1964 [1936]), 18, 25.

5. Keynes, *General Theory*, 30.

6. Bureau of the Census, U.S. Department of Commerce, *Historical Statistics of the United States, Colonial Times to 1970*, no. 1 (Washington, DC: GPO, 1975): 1001, 1002, 1021.

7. I am deeply indebted to my former colleague, Huw Pill (who is now an official at the European Central Bank), for helping me to see that Keynes viewed expansionary fiscal policy fundamentally as a coordination device.

8. When central bank officials believe the economy is overheating (or is on the verge of overheating) because actual GDP exceeds (or is about to exceed) their estimate of potential GDP, they will normally raise the short-term interest under their control (i.e., tighten monetary policy) in order to fight or preempt inflation. As a result, considerable weight rests on the central bank's estimates of potential output and its trajectory going forward. If, for example, actual output is growing at 4 percent per year and the central bank has estimated potential output growth at 3 percent per year, it is far more likely to tighten monetary policy (i.e., raise the short-term interest rate) than if it believed potential output was growing at 4.5 percent per year (which would suggest the economy had additional room to grow without overheating).

9. As is well known, bond prices and bond yields move in opposite directions. When many people want to buy bonds, this will obviously bid up their price. But this will also drive down their yields. If the price of a $100 bond that was to pay $110 at the end of the year (i.e., 10 percent interest) is bid up to $105, then the effective yield is driven down to just 4.8 percent (i.e., [110 − 105]/105). Another way to look at this is that as more people want to buy bonds, a greater supply of investment funds becomes available, which in turn means that the price of those investment funds (the interest rate) should fall.

Chapter Four

1. *Journals of the Continental Congress, 1774–1789*, ed. Worthington C. Ford et al. (Washington, DC, 1904–37), 29: 499–500.

2. *Journals of the Continental Congress* 30 (1786): 162–163. The Board of Treasury also noted that a "Dollar containing this number of Grains of fine Silver, will be worth as much as the New Spanish Dollars." The so-called New Spanish Dollar, or Spanish milled dollar, was a foreign coin that was widely used as money in the United States at the time.

3. *Journal of the Senate* 1 (January 12, 1792): 374.

4. Although attempts to measure the trajectory of prices—by tracking the prices of a broad basket of goods—can be traced all the way back to 1806, "the first serious attempt to summarize comprehensive price data for the United States in the form of index numbers was made by Horatio C. Burchard, Director of the Mint" in 1881. Bureau of the Census, U.S. Department of Commerce, *Historical Statistics of the United States, Colonial Times to 1970*, no. 1 (Washington, DC: GPO, 1975): 183.

5. Irving Fisher, "A Remedy for the Rising Cost of Living: Standardizing the Dollar," *American Economic Review* 3, no. 1 (Supplement, March 1913): 20.

6. Albert Gordon, interview by author, New York City, October 22, 2003.

7. The European Central Bank might be said to have adopted a weak version of inflation targeting, based on an "inflation objective" rather than a hard target. Developed countries that had adopted even stronger versions of inflation targeting included Sweden, Britain, and New Zealand.

8. Quoted in Eldar Shafir, Peter Diamond, and Amos Tversky, "Money Illusion," *Quarterly Journal of Economics*, 112, no. 2 (May 1997): 341–342.

9. The new Chairman of the Federal Reserve, Ben Bernanke (confirmed in 2006), was thought to favor explicit inflation targeting. By contrast, his predecessor, Alan Greenspan, had never announced an explicit inflation target.

Chapter Five

1. This chapter is drawn (with some modifications) from David Moss and Sarah Brennan, "National Economic Accounting: Past, Present, and Future," Case 703-026 (Boston: Harvard Business School, 2002).

2. Although used goods are not included in GDP, the sale of a used good is often associated with the production of a new service, which is included. The used items sold on eBay, for example, are not counted as part of GDP. However, the commission paid to eBay for making an online auction is counted as a new service and therefore included. It is also worth noting that the components of GDP do reflect the net transfer of used goods across sectors of the economy. Consumption, for example, includes the purchase of used rental cars by households (Bureau of Economic Analysis, *A Guide to the NIPAs*, updated 31 August 2001, http://www.bea.gov/bea/an/nipaguid.htm, M.8, M.9).

3. Investment also includes the wages and salaries a business may pay to people hired as part of an investment project. For example, if a café builds a specialized high-tech coffee maker, the wages of the computer programmer will show up in investment.

4. Shelby B. Herman, "Fixed Assets and Consumer Durable Goods," *Survey of Current Business* (April 2000): 18.

5. U.S. Department of Commerce, *National Income, Supplement to the Survey of Current Business*, July 1947 (Washington, DC: GPO, 1947), 11.

6. Under the GDP definition, "net exports" is basically the balance on goods and services (from the balance of payments accounts). Under the GNP definition, by contrast, "net exports" approximately equals the balance on goods and services *plus* net income payments (again, from the balance of payments accounts).

7. World Development Indicators database, http://devdata.worldbank.org.ezp2.harvard.edu/dataonline (accessed November 2006). Note, GNP estimates were labeled GNI.

8. In the United States, the growth rate of the GDP deflator was often (but not always) similar in magnitude to the growth rate of the Consumer Price Index (CPI), which was constructed by tracking changes in the sales price of a fixed basket of *consumer* goods.

9. Arthur F. Burns, "The Measurement of the Physical Volume of Production," *Quarterly Journal of Economics* 44, no. 2 (February 1930): 242–262.

10. Karl Whelan, "A Guide to the Use of Chain Aggregated NIPA Data," Federal Reserve Board, Division of Research and Statistics, June 2000, 4–5, www.federalreserve.gov/Pubs/feds/2000/200035/200035 pap.pdf.

11. J. Steven Landefeld and Bruce T. Grimm, "A Note on the Impact of Hedonics and Computers on Real GDP," *Survey of Current Business* (December 2000): 17–22.

12. J. Steven Landefeld and Robert P. Parker, "BEA's Chain Index, Time Series, and Measures of Long-Term Economic Growth," *Survey of Current Business* (May 1997): 58–68.

13. World Bank, "About the International Comparison Group," available at www.worldbank.org/data/icp/abouticp.htm; "About the International Comparison of Prices Program," available at http://pwt.econ.upenn.edu.

14. Note that net imports (i.e., IM – EX) on the GDP accounts is approximately equal to the current account deficit (excluding net income and transfers) on the balance of payments.

Chapter Six

1. In practice, since official agencies don't pick up every cross-border transaction, the "errors and omissions" category is necessary to ensure that the various parts of the BOP statement do indeed sum to zero.

2. This example was inspired by a classroom exercise my colleague Louis T. Wells developed.

Chapter Seven

1. Jennifer Hughes, "Online Effect Rebalances the FX Equation," *Financial Times* (July 30–31, 2005): 11.

Conclusion

1. Federal Reserve Chairman Alan Greenspan is often credited with coining the term "irrational exuberance" in a speech entitled "The Challenge of Central Banking in a Democratic Society," which he delivered at the American Enterprise Institute for Public Policy Research in Washington, D.C., on December 5, 1996. See also Robert Shiller, *Irrational Exuberance* (Princeton: Princeton University Press, 2000).

INDEX

Index

direct investment. *See* foreign direct investment (FDI)
discount rate, 62, 63*f*, 91–92, 94, 135
discount window, 64, 91–92
division of labor, efficiency and, 165–166*n*5
dollar. *See also* currency; money; money supply (M); exchange rates
 proposed standardization of, 90–91, 169*n*5
 Spanish milled dollar, 169*n*2
 as unit of account, 88, 89, 169*n*1
double counting, 10, 100–101
downward spiral, 73, 137

eBay, 170*n*2
economic growth
 productivity and, 21–22, 165–166*n*5
 sources of, 19–23, 165–166*n*5
economic relationships, theory vs. practice, 65–66, 140–141
economic shock, 72
education and productivity, 21
efficiency
 division of labor and, 165–166*n*5
 increases in, economic growth and, 19, 20
 reduced, through wage and price controls, 70
 Total Factor Productivity (TFP) as measure of, 20, 22, 22*n*
"elastic" money supply, 91–92

errors and omissions in balance of payments, 116, 118, 121, 122*t*, 123, 171*n*1
Eurodollar accounts, 167*n*9
European Central Bank, 95, 168*n*7, 170*n*7
EX. *See* exports (EX)
exchange, money used to facilitate, 33, 166*n*1
exchange-rate models, 127, 128–129
exchange-rate peg. *See* fixed exchange rate; pegged exchange rate
exchange rates, 1, 4, 35*n*, 35–36, 37*f*, 37–38, 38*f*, 47–54, 89–95,125–131
 bimetallic standard, 89
 and currency crises. *See* currency crises
 current account balance and, 125–126, 130, 131
 determination of, 125–131
 effects of money on. *See* money
 expectations and, 83
 fixed, 89–90, 92–93. *See also* exchange rates, pegged
 floating, 93*n*, 93–95
 forecasting, unpredictability of, 130, 131
 foreign investment and, 52–53
 gold standard. *See* gold standard
 inflation and. *See* real exchange rate
 interest rates and, 128–129, 131
 monetary policy goals and, 59–60, 136

credibility of, wage and price
controls and, 70–71
role in early U.S. monetary
system, 88–89
government bonds, 75, 81–82.
See also open market
operations
government expenditure (G), in
GDP accounting, 10, 11, 14*t*,
101, 102, 103*t*, 110, 111,
111*t*, 112. *See also* GDP
accounting
"autonomous" increase in,
77–79, 78*f*, 82
deficit spending. *See* deficit
spending; fiscal policy
government-led investment, 23,
29
government saving (budget surplus), 110, 111, 111*t*
government spending. *See* government expenditure (G)
Great Depression. *See also*
depression
causes of, 23–24
effects on cost of borrowing,
74–75, 75*t*
gold standard and, 92–93,
170*n*6
Greenspan, Alan, 170*n*9, 172*n*1
Grimm, Bruce T., 171*n*11
gross domestic product (GDP),
8–11, 14*t*, 99–113,
133–134. *See also* GDP
accounting; national output
actual and potential GDP compared, 72, 168–169*n*8
comparison of nominal vs. real
GDP, 39–43, 40*t*, 41*t*, 42*t*,
106–108, 135

components of, 10–11,
101–102, 103*t*
controlling for inflation in
measurement of, 41,
106–108, 135
vs. domestic expenditure,
112
GNP compared, 105–106
historical and cross-country
comparisons, 106–109
increase in, income multiplier
and, 76–78, 78*f*
items excluded from, 101, 102,
105, 170*n*2
PPP-adjusted estimates of GDP
per capita, 109, 109*t*,
171*n*13
real. *See* gross domestic product, comparison of nominal
vs. real GDP; real GDP
standard definition of, 9, 101
gross national product (GNP),
105–106, 171*n*6

Harvard Business School, ix, 3,
22, 92
Herman, Shelby B., 170*n*4
Honda, 11
Hoover, Herbert, 23–24, 166*n*6
"hot money," 118. *See also* port-
folio investment
Hughes, Jennifer, 172*n*1
Hume, David, 33, 166*n*1

I. *See* investment
IM. *See* imports (IM)
IMF (International Monetary
Fund), 117

ABOUT THE AUTHOR

David A. Moss is the John G. McLean Professor at Harvard Business School. He earned his BA from Cornell University (1986) and his PhD from Yale University (1992). After leaving Yale, Moss served as a senior economist at Abt Associates, a public policy consulting firm based in Cambridge, Massachusetts. He joined the Business School faculty in July 1993.

Professor Moss has written two previous books: *Socializing Security: Progressive-Era Economists and the Origins of American Social Policy* (Harvard University Press, 1996) and *When All Else Fails: Government as the Ultimate Risk Manager* (Harvard University Press, 2002). The latter explores the government's pivotal role as a risk manager in policies ranging from limited liability and bankruptcy law to social insurance and federal disaster relief. Moss has also published numerous articles, book chapters, and case studies, and over the past four years headed the popular first-year MBA course "Business, Government, and the International Economy" at Harvard Business School.

Professor Moss is a member of the National Academy of Social Insurance. Recent honors include the Robert F. Greenhill Award, the Editors' Prize from the *American Bankruptcy Law Journal*, the Student Association Faculty Award for outstanding teaching at the Harvard Business School, and the American Risk and Insurance Association's 2004 Kulp-Wright Book Award for "the most influential text published on the economics of risk management and insurance."